DON'T FORGET!

DON'T FORGET!

Easy Exercises
for a Better Memory
at Any Age

Danielle C. Lapp

McGRAW-HILL BOOK COMPANY

New York   St. Louis   San Francisco   Bogotá
Guatemala   Hamburg   Lisbon
Madrid   Mexico   Montreal   Panama   Paris   San Juan
São Paulo   Tokyo   Toronto

1 2 3 4 5 6 7 8 9 F G R F G R 8 7 6

ISBN 0-07-036373-0{H.C.}
ISBN 0-07-036369-2{PBK.}

LIBRARY OF CONGRESS CATALOGING-IN-PUBLICATION DATA

Lapp, Danielle C.
  Don't forget!
  1. Memory—Problems, exercises, etc.   2. Attention—
Problems, exercises, etc.   3. Mnemonics—Problems,
exercises, etc.   I. Title.
BF371.L256 1987   153.1'4   86-20001

ISBN 0-07-036373-0{H.C.}
ISBN 0-07-036369-2{PBK.}

EDITING SUPERVISOR: MARGERY LUHRS
BOOK DESIGN BY PATRICE FODERO

In memory of John Lapp,
who filled my life with happy memories.

Acknowledgments

This book could not have been written without the moral support of Dr. Jerome Yesavage. He gave me the opportunity to experiment with ideas and was always confident about the results, encouraging me to write and use the word processor. Thanks to his help, I completed the manuscript sooner than expected. Our secretary, Emily Gere, deserves my gratitude for her patience and kindness while I was mastering the word processor. She also proved to be a living dictionary of the American language.

Credit should be given to those who contributed ideas, especially to Dr. Jim Westphal in the section on mental attitudes. I quote others individually throughout the book. Unfortunately, I cannot name all those who made it possible for me to complete the task, but I must mention Marie Louise Frealle and Paul Watzlawick. My friend Linda West Eckhart in particular instilled in me her incorrigible optimism throughout the project.

I would like to thank Ken Stuart for believing in the manuscript from the moment I handed it to him. I would also like to thank Lisa Frost, who edited the manuscript with such competence and loving care.

Contents

Foreword

This book by Danielle Lapp has been developed over her several years of experience teaching memory improvement techniques to a wide variety of people. The techniques in this book are based on scientific studies done with members of the department of psychiatry and behavioral sciences of the Stanford University School of Medicine. These studies have documented the fact that the techniques work. A reasonable amount of interest paid to Mrs. Lapp's ideas will be repaid tenfold by improved concentration and memory capacity. I hope you will catch her enthusiasm for this material, enjoy doing the exercises, and rapidly make progress in improving your memory.

Jerome A. Yesavage, M.D.
Associate Professor of
Psychiatry and Behavioral Sciences
Stanford University School of Medicine

Preface

"The *wish* to learn is diffuse and general. The *will* to learn is concentrated and specific. The wish to learn means that we repeat a thing again and again hoping for something to happen. The will to learn means that we dig down and analyze. . . . So, the will to learn means an intelligent and persistent search for the conditions of improvement, and an intelligent and persistent concentration upon them."

Professor James L. Mursell (Columbia University)

You may at times have wished you had a better memory, but not knowing how to go about it, you may have given up with the thought that nothing could be done. In fact, all it takes to guarantee success is curiosity and the will to try a specific method which has proved to be of value. This book is the result of 8 years of experience teaching memory training to people above 55 years of age. Whether you are in this age group or younger, you can benefit from it because of its approach. It follows the natural way memory works, from perception and emotion to selective attention to analytical organized thinking. It takes into account the latest research findings and shows in a simple manner how to apply them to everyday life. If you have ever asked yourself, "What can I do, practically, to improve my memory?" you will appreciate the suggestions at the end of each chapter. I structured the course around the following questions:

1. What gets in the way of memory?
2. How can attention be improved?
3. How can memory systems (mnemonics) be explained in a practical and simple form?

In Part I, "Clearing the Way to Concentration," you will learn how memory works, what prevents it from functioning normally, and how you can easily remove these obstacles.

In Part II, "Improving Concentration," you will become more observant and selective, making sure you get a good *recording* of what you want to remember.

In Part III, "Improving Organization," you will learn how to prompt *recall*, which is the biggest problem at any age, but more so as people get older.

By the end of the concentration training, you will feel better about your memory because you will be making conscious recordings of what you want to remember. You will have noticed that most memory problems are not *retention* problems but *attention* problems. After this initial training, including exercises and practical application, you will be ready to use systems (mnemonics) because you will be familiar with the methods that underlie them. I have avoided presenting dry and abstract information because the purpose here is to *train* memory. Quick Reviews follow each chapter to provide a concise synthesis for better recall. By the end of the book you will have developed habits and assimilated techniques which help memory. There is no doubt that memory training works. It is much easier than you think and enjoyable, too.

The aim of this book is to show you how to gain control over your memory. You will leave behind the feeling of helplessness which may have made you lose self-confidence. You will learn how to combine your emotional and intellectual resources. By consciously integrating everything you have at your disposal—your sensory awareness and your imagination as well as your selective organizational skills—you will be recording sharp personal memories. You will then have the satisfaction of knowing that you can remember what you decide to remember.

Finally, whenever you forget something, you will understand why and will more readily accept the imperfections of human memory. You may not get the ideal memory you dream of, but you will improve your memory beyond your wildest expectations.

DON'T FORGET!

Introduction

How to Use This Book

You can use this book to improve your own memory or as a source of practical ideas to help someone else with memory problems. Set your own pace according to your needs. Define your goals and work toward them, giving yourself enough time to apply the new learning. For instance, you may especially want to remember names. Read the whole book first but concentrate on the relevant chapter and watch your progress in this area. Since it is a practical manual, you will learn how to apply the principles to your life. Just reading this book will help, because the method entails learning about the memory process and developing habits that facilitate memory.

If you want to practice more thoroughly and achieve even better results, there are exercises at the end of each chapter that will reinforce what you have read and help you carry it into your daily activities. You will see the payoff right away, and you will have fun with the material, too. Think about applying what you have learned in small ways throughout the day; just by being more relaxed, more aware, more observant, more positive, and more selective, you will improve your memory.

For maximum improvement, I suggest the following three steps:

1. *Read the chapter* first and review it with the Quick Review.

2. *Do the exercises* that follow the text. They are designed
    to do the following:

    • *Train your mind* to apply methods that facilitate
      memorization. They will teach you to do the mental
      operations recognized as effective and put you on
      the right track so that you can continue on your own.

    • *Provide examples* of how to apply these methods to
      your daily life.

    • *Facilitate generalization* of the principles behind
      these methods by showing how they work when ap-
      plied to other areas.

3. *Keep a diary* to help you follow up and apply what you
    have practiced in the exercises to your daily life, which
    is your ultimate goal. Write only about "memory"—
    about your attempts to apply the techniques and how
    you went about it. Keeping track of your progress can
    be very rewarding.

Buy a notebook; use one side for the exercises and the other
for the diary. Keep it next to this book and try to work a little
every day. Persevere; do not give up before you have given it
your best try. This will take time at first. No one has ever
broken inefficient habits in a day or learned a skill without
training. Memory is a skill that you have to practice daily, but
this is a pleasant task that will bring you immediate rewards. If
you are committed to improving your memory, you will succeed with the help of this book.

Testing Your Memory

Before reading further, you may want to test yourself. Here
is a unique opportunity to get an objective evaluation in the
privacy of your own home. You will know where you started
from and will be able to gauge your progress by comparing your
first performance with later ones. (Keep your answers.) Relax

and do your best. You may do better than you expected. If worse comes to worst, you will be motivated to take memory training seriously.

You will need a pad of paper, a pencil, and for certain tests a kitchen timer. The last test cannot be done alone: Either skip it or ask a friend to test you. When testing yourself, answer one question at a time. Do not read ahead, because the tests are meant to be disclosed in sequence. Make sure you will not be disturbed for some time. Choose a pleasant, well-lit room free from noise and interference. Good luck!

Identifying Your Memory Problems

The following questionnaire will allow you to identify the areas in which you have memory problems. At the end of the book, after you have finished the training, you will answer the same questionnaire. Chances are good that your answers will not be the same. It will be rewarding to gauge your progress. How good or bad do you feel your memory is in the following areas?

		Excellent			*Average*			*Poor*
a.	My memory in general	1	2	3	4	5	6	7
b.	Names and faces	1	2	3	4	5	6	7
c.	Appointments	1	2	3	4	5	6	7
d.	Where I put things, e.g., keys	1	2	3	4	5	6	7
e.	Words	1	2	3	4	5	6	7
f.	Things I have read	1	2	3	4	5	6	7
g.	Remembering what I was doing before an interruption	1	2	3	4	5	6	7
h.	What people tell me	1	2	3	4	5	6	7
i.	Places I have been	1	2	3	4	5	6	7
j.	Directions and instructions	1	2	3	4	5	6	7

Memory and Mood Tests

1. Attention Test: Digit Span Read the following lines of numbers one at a time, spending about a second on each while

Figure I-1

hiding the others with your hand. After each line, stop, look up, say the numbers aloud in reverse order, and then write them down in that order.

example: 6 8 0 ⎯⎯⎯⎯→ say without looking 0 8 6

write 0 8 6

```
1 9 8
3 2 8 4
5 6 1 9
1 9 3 6 7
8 2 5 7 4
9 7 6 2 3 8
5 1 8 3 9 4
```

2. Attention Test: Scanning For this exercise you will need good eyesight. Put on your eyeglasses if you wear any and sit under a good light. In Figure I-1 you will draw a line through every letter Z you can find in 30 seconds. Set a timer, start at the upper left, and stop as soon as the time is up. Count the number of Z's you found. Look again and try to find some more.

3. Visual Memory: Recognition of Abstract Figures Look at Figure I-2 for 30 seconds. Then wait 2 minutes before turning the page. Turn the page, look at Figure I-3, and mark an X under each figure you recognize. Check yourself by comparing the figures you marked with the originals.

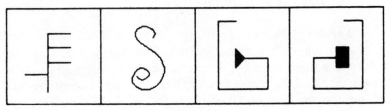

Figure I-2

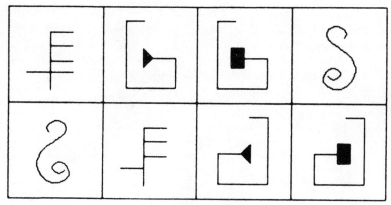

Figure I-3

4. Visual Memory: Imagery Look at the following letters for 30 seconds, trying to remember them as they appear on the page.

O   R   D
K   N   S
L   C   A

Cover the letters.

1. Write down the letters exactly as you saw them.
2. Cover what you just wrote and try to say which letters formed an X; that is, give the letters in a diagonal order.
3. How did you remember the letters?

   • Did you visualize them?

   • Did you analyze them? How?

5. Faces and Names In Figure I-4 you will see 12 pictures of faces, each with a name written underneath. Look at one picture at a time, spending 1 minute on each, trying to remember the face and the name. Cover all the pictures except the one you will be working on. When you are finished, turn the page and in Figure I-5 write down the names corresponding to the

faces you will find there. You have a maximum of 6 minutes to do so. Do the whole series at once without interruption.

6. Lists Study the following list of 20 words for 3 minutes. Try to remember as many words as you can. Turn the page and wait 2 minutes. Then write down all the items you remember. Check yourself, writing the number of correct words for future reference. If you remembered the list in order, congratulations! Try to determine how you went about it.

1. House	6. Wagon	11. Lamp	16. Policeman
2. Rifle	7. Telephone	12. Train	17. Tie
3. Chipmunk	8. Dog	13. Towel	18. Ivy
4. Elbow	9. Shirt	14. Bee	19. Toes
5. Wisecrack	10. Tomato	15. Cow	20. Bridge

7. Reading Retention Read the following paragraph carefully, trying to remember as much of it as possible. When you're through, turn the page and write everything you can remember on your pad. Check what you've written against the text. Do this line by line, and you will not omit anything.

FOLLOW-UP Tomorrow write down what you remember of the story and compare it with today's results. Try again a week later and see how you do.

Toward the end of the Second World War, Hitler asked the few social scientists left in Germany to find out why people made bad decisions. When they reported that the main cause was mental fatigue, he asked them for a list of the signs of mental fatigue. Then he issued an order: Any officer showing signs of mental fatigue should immediately be sent on vacation. Fortunately for the world, he did not apply the order to himself.

B. F. Skinner

1. James
   Howard

2. Dixie
   Vierra

5. Florence
   Izumie

6. Bob
   Zeiss

9. Rand
   Lenhart

10. Martha
    McHaffey

Figure I-4

3. Carlos
   Greaves

4. Linda
   Kaiser

7. Pat
   Dilkian

8. Gary
   Wood

11. Bernard
    Williams

12. Enid
    Chados

Figure I-4 (cont.)

Figure I-5

Figure I-5 (cont.)

8. Mood Measure   Mood and memory are closely related. Answer the following questions yes or no. Be spontaneous and move on quickly to the next question.

Choose the best answer for how you felt over the past week:

1. Are you basically satisfied with your life?
2. Have you dropped many of your activities and interests?
3. Do you feel that your life is empty?
4. Do you often get bored?
5. Are you in good spirits most of the time?
6. Are you afraid that something bad is going to happen to you?
7. Do you feel happy most of the time?
8. Do you often feel helpless?
9. Do you prefer to stay at home rather than going out and doing new things?
10. Do you feel you have more problems with memory than most?
11. Do you think it is wonderful to be alive now?
12. Do you feel pretty worthless the way you are now?
13. Do you feel full of energy?
14. Do you feel your situation is hopeless?
15. Do you think most people are better off than you are?

9. Visual Memory Test   Ask a friend to give you the following test. Have him or her read it first so that he or she gets a good understanding of the whole test.

The object is to remember a number of items seen for a brief period of time. Ask your friend to leave the room. Take 15 different objects of general use (for example, a bottle, a box, a vase, a book) and place them on a table. Separate the objects but do not arrange them in a row. Invite your friend back into the room and direct him or her to look at each object for 5 seconds. Then cover the objects with a cloth and ask your friend the following questions. Have your friend write down the answers as you go.

- Name as many objects as you can remember.
- How many objects were there?
- Describe each object. What color was it? What texture did it have?
- Where was the object placed on the table?

Conclusion

How did you do? If you are not too happy with your results, there is hope. Just by taking these tests, you have already learned something about memory: Attention, imagery, organization, and mood all play major roles. You will see why and how in the following chapters. Right now, score your test. You may have done better than you think.

How to Score Your Test

The following averages are based on the results of people beginning our retraining courses.

1. Digit Span:
   5 correct is average.
   6 correct is very good.
2. Scanning:
   10 Z's identified is average.
   11 to 14 is good.
   15 or more is excellent.
3. Recognition of Abstract Figures:
   3 on the four-item test is average.
4. Imagery:
   4 of 5 in their correct places is average.

5. Faces and Names:

   6 of 12 correct is average.

   7 or 8 is good, and more than 8 is excellent.

6. Lists:

   12 of 20 is average.

   13 or 14 is good, and more than 14 is excellent.

7. Reading Retention: The test is scored by counting the number of items correctly remembered. Each one of the following ideas counts for one item correct.

   1. Toward the end of the Second World War,

   2. Hitler asked the few social scientists left in Germany

   3. to find out why people made bad decisions.

   4. When they reported that the main cause was mental fatigue,

   5. he asked them for a list of the signs of mental fatigue.

   6. Then he issued an order:

   7. Any officer showing signs of mental fatigue

   8. should immediately be sent on vacation.

   9. Fortunately for the world, he did not apply the order to himself.

   10. (B. F. Skinner)

   7 items correct is average.

   8 correct is good.

   More than 8 is excellent.

   If you check yourself a day later,

   4 items correct is average.

   5 or 6 correct is good.

   More than 6 is excellent.

8. Mood Measure: The following answers count one point:

1.	*no*	*6.*	*yes*	*11.*	*no*
2.	*yes*	*7.*	*no*	*12.*	*yes*
3.	*yes*	*8.*	*yes*	*13.*	*no*
4.	*yes*	*9.*	*yes*	*14.*	*yes*
5.	*no*	*10.*	*yes*	*15.*	*yes*

A score higher than 5 points may indicate a depression and should be brought to the attention of your physician.

9. Visual Memory:

6 of 10 items is average.

7 is good, and 8 is excellent.

What Do Your Test Results Mean?

The point of these tests was to highlight your strengths and weaknesses. Chances are that you did not score in the excellent range on every test. (If you did, pass this book on to a friend who may need it.) Most likely, some areas of weakness appeared. One theme of this book is the difference between memory (retention) and attention. Examination of your results may indicate that attention is your weak point; this should encourage you to spend as much time as possible on the attention and concentration exercises. Conversely, you may find that memory was more of a problem; this should lead you to pay particular attention to the chapters on specific memory techniques. As we progress in the book, much will be made of the different types of memory tested and exercises will allow you to test yourself so that you can measure your progress. After finishing the book you can do these tests again and compare the results.

PART 1

Clearing the Way to Concentration

CHAPTER 1

A Few Facts about Memory

"If you don't have the motivation, you are not going to acquire the knowledge base to be successful."

Bill Chase (University of Pittsburgh)

When we say, "I cannot remember names, places I have been, things I have to do," we should ask ourselves whether we have really tried to remember those things. Chances are that we did not really need to remember them or did not make the necessary effort to do so. We unconsciously select the important things to keep in storage and discard the rest. Most of the time we are on "automatic," and we do not do anything consciously to ensure that we are leaving a memory trace. Amazingly, most of the time it works without one's conscious cooperation. Memory problems arise when useful information is not retained or recalled, causing difficulties in everyday life.

If, for one reason or another, you fail to perform the necessary mental operations to record what you want to remember, do not despair. You need only understand what takes place unawares when you remember and when you forget. Then you can switch from "automatic" to "manual," making memories happen rather than waiting for them to happen. By becoming aware of your passivity, you can correct this trend toward forgetfulness. You can learn how to be selective and more efficient in concentrating precisely on what is important for a particular task. You can become more open to observation and use associations to gather details.

19

You will gain control over your memory as you learn how to ensure a proper recording in your mind of what you want to remember. In order to facilitate recall, you will use everything you have at your disposal: your senses, your intellect (organizational skills), and your imagination. In doing so you will improve your attention, which is often at fault.

The aim of this book is to teach you how to do consciously what your mind does not do unconsciously. The exercises will allow you to test yourself and find out what you do right and what you do wrong.

Only when something does not work to our satisfaction do we look into its mechanism. Memory is not an innate mysterious wonder machine functioning independently of our will or control. If it were, most people would despair, since exceptional memories are extremely rare. Memory is a mechanism we have to understand in order to make the most of it. As children we were never taught how to memorize or how memory works. Thus, we managed by trial and error, with a few individuals doing instinctively better than the rest. The method most commonly taught in schools is repetition. However, there are many other methods which, combined with repetition, will give more effective results for memorizing many kinds of things, be they names or appointments or other useful information.

First, let us take a look at the conditions in which memory operates. A brief remark about human nature points in the right direction: What prompts a person to do something is a system of reinforcements or rewards, since anything one undertakes requires effort. We constantly have to adapt to changes in the environment, but we adjust our behavior only if it is worth it, that is, if we get personal satisfaction. If we do, everything goes smoothly: We learn and remember without suffering from the effort involved. Actually, the task appears effortless, like enjoying a good game of chess or golf. Memory follows the same pattern.

At the root, there is a *need* or *interest*. No one forgets to eat or go to work. The rewards are obvious and surpass the inconveniences. Need or interest brings about the *motivation* to pay *attention* and *concentrate* on what it is one wants to remember. *Concentration* is sustained attention, and without it there can be no sure recording of memories. How efficiently one can concentrate plays a big role. Equally important is what the mind does in this ideal state of concentration. *Organization* is the ultimate requirement for a good memory.

The pattern of memory will be best remembered as a chain made of these essential links:

NEED
or
INTEREST → MOTIVATION → ATTENTION → CONCENTRATION → ORGANIZATION

Forgetting occurs whenever this chain is broken. When new things come along that seem more important at the moment, they monopolize our attention, and the rest fades into the background. As circumstances in life bring them back again, we remember. Forgetting is part of the mechanism of memory. It is necessary to forget many things momentarily in order to attend to what we are doing. It may be sad to think that we have forgotten most of what we learned at school, but we do remember what we use in our daily lives: reading and counting, for instance. Besides, if you had to go back to school and train for a new career, you would recall many of the basics you have forgotten, and learning would be easier because you would find a frame of reference in your memory bank. You would not be starting from scratch, which proves more difficult as people get older. Perhaps this is one of the best reasons for a good education: an investment in *recognition,* a type of memory that is not easily altered by age or circumstances. However, if you consider how flimsy learning can be, you cannot always be sure that the information was properly registered for long-term retention. You may not recognize many things you learned by rote and never used. The memory traces may not have been very sharp or may have been erased in the case of information you did not care about.

What happens when a person forgets? Looking at the memory chain, you can see that there are three potential causes of link breakage: lack of need, interest, or motivation; lack of attention or concentration; and lack of organization. Any one or a combination of these may be responsible for poor memory. This explains why *anxiety* and *depression* are the villains most often blamed for memory problems: When we are depressed, we lose interest and motivation, making it difficult or impossible to sustain attention; when we are anxious, our attention is captured by our anxiety and we are unable to attend to anything else. Without concentration, we cannot hope to organize our thoughts for efficient recall.

Your first concern should be to determine which links are weak in your memory chain. Since you're motivated enough to read this book, your problem is probably either attention or retention. Technically speaking, a retention deficit is the only true memory problem: Although one may be motivated, pay attention, and try to remember, one forgets because the memories were not properly registered and stored for easy recall. The information got in, but it is hard to retrieve. Organization will help anyone with a retention problem. However, most memory complaints stem from attention deficits: Nothing is recorded in the first place, hence there is nothing to recall. How can you be sure you have recorded something? You cannot be sure, but you can get a pretty good idea by analyzing the circumstances in which you were trying to record the information. In order to understand memory failures, you must know how your environment and your emotions influence your ability to leave a quality memory trace. You can expect memory lapses when your emotions take over and when the situation does not allow you to sustain attention. This is the case

- When rushing
- When anxious
- When under stress or pressure
- When distracted
- When interrupted
- When interferences or digressions occur
- When emotions run high or low (elation or depression)
- When self-absorbed

- When tired or drowsy (drugs)
- When your resistance is down (illness)
- When in familiar surroundings
- When making automatic gestures
- When habit prevails
- When you cannot make sense of the message

To believe that your memory can function in these circumstances is to believe in miracles. Don't count on it! There is no point blaming yourself or your memory when it is impossible to control you attention or when there is no time to organize and process information. Sometimes a person cannot avoid being anxious, distracted, or rushed. Don't expect much of yourself unless you can change the circumstances, i.e., unless you can pause, relax, and focus. In some cases this simply cannot be done, for example, when rushing to catch a train.

Whether young, middle aged, or older, there are times we remember and times we forget. We express frustration with words, which we use as weapons to browbeat ourselves. I suggest that you modify your vocabulary in accordance with the situation. Instead of saying frequently, "I forgot," try saying, "I cannot think of it now," "I was not paying attention," "I didn't hear you," "I didn't listen," "It did not register," or "I didn't make it a point to remember." As you vary your vocabulary, you acknowledge the various situations which may cause forgetfulness. You will abandon guilt feelings and stop blaming your memory at every opportunity. Be happy when you catch yourself remembering something in the nick of time, as is the case when you notice your coat in the car after locking the door. Your reflex of shutting the door was so fast that there was no time to pause and think. Remembering a few seconds later was all you could do under the circumstances. Paradoxically, we often say "I forgot" at the very moment we remember. We are so impatient with our memory that we don't give it a chance. Instead, congratulate yourself, saying, "I'm glad I remembered; so what if it took me a few seconds." Reserve the word "forgot" for episodes with more dramatic consequences.

The more you know about memory function, the kinder you will be to yourself. With the help of this book, you will learn how to gain control over your memory by making conscious, quality recordings. Your chances of recall will be increased a thousandfold by the methods of organization you will soon master. In a nutshell, here is what it is all about.

Recording Information

Imagine that you want to record a message or a song. First, you want to make sure your equipment is in working condition. Your doctor will be able to detect the fairly rare biological deteriorations that cause serious memory loss. Second, you'll need to check all sources of interference that are likely to blur your recording and make it hard to decode; that is, you want to eliminate all thoughts not connected to what you want to remember. *Concentration* is the key to memorization. You must focus your attention on what you want to record and spend the necessary time and effort. As you develop a "photographic memory," this should result in a clear *image,* or a concrete representation of what you want to store in your memory recorder. To form this image, you will use your sensory perceptions to their fullest. Too often we see but do not look, feel without being aware of it, hear casually without listening. By paying attention you will ensure that all your channels, sensory and intellectual, are open and active. The making of the image involves both imagination and intellect. By associating image and message, you will make a better recording on your memory track. Thus *association* is the third key word, forming a mnemonic easy to remember: CIA for *concentration, image, association.*

Recalling Information

The clearer the recording, the easier the recall. That is why it is important to spend some time and effort on the CIA process, which ensures proper recording. When you cannot remember something at one time but can do so at another time, it is because some exterior factor has triggered an association which in turn has brought the memory back to your consciousness. When you see, hear, taste, smell, or touch something and are reminded of something else (a place, a person, or a mood), you have responded to a stimulus. This stimulus-response mechanism prompts recall without voluntary effort, with one impression triggering the next in a domino effect. You can gain control of your recall mechanisms by voluntarily defining the stimulus and reinforcing it with specific techniques. For example, if you often forget your umbrella, try this: You know you are going to see your front door on your way out, right? Think "front door" and visualize it with your umbrella open right in front of it. Spend a few seconds on this image association. Whenever you see the door, the umbrella will pop out, reminding you of it. For every image association you will make, you will have to define a stimulus you cannot miss seeing. It will act as a visual prompter. The secret to success lies in spending at least 10 seconds visualizing the two items together in a single image.

Image forming and association help in the retrieval process, which is the most difficult part of remembering. First, they guarantee a deep recording into long-term memory; second, they act as cues prompting recall. As one ages, the capacity for retrieving information decreases. The following techniques will help you in the process of recording and recalling anything you may want to remember. Studies have shown that usually it is not so much the storage system of memory which is at fault but rather the recall system. Free recall is very inefficient, whereas prompted organized recall is quite efficient. Planting cues at the time of recording guarantees efficient recall. Learning how to cue oneself is the true art of memory.

These techniques are based on the assumption that memory is a skill rather than a gift. Even gifted artists must practice, though, since a gift is just raw potential, a promising beginning. As the old saying goes, "Practice makes perfect," or at least brings us close to our idea of perfection.

CHAPTER 2

How Memory Works

"We have all forgot more than we remember."

Thomas Fuller (1732)

The *Oxford English Dictionary* defines "memory" as "the faculty of remembering." Like every mental process, it is a complex matter. Remembering something, we push aside other memories, which are at least momentarily forgotten. Overall, since we forget more than we remember, it is the selection and quality of our memories that count. We usually do not complain if we remember what we need to remember. Actually, we should be glad to forget many things. Many people with extraordinary memories are not happier; they wish they could forget! In normal memory function there is a healthy balance. As Alexander Chase put it, in a true paradox, "Memory is the thing you forget with." You will soon see why. To understand how people remember, we are going to look at several models which describe memory from different perspectives. Each one is complementary and will add to your understanding of memory function.

Physiological Models

Anatomical Models

The anatomy of memory in the brain is somewhat diffuse, though most memory function is centered in the hippocampus, which is on the temporal lobes on both sides of the brain. If either lobe is damaged, it is still possible for memory to function, but if both are destroyed, so is the capacity to remember.

Neurochemical Models

In the hippocampus, the neurotransmitter acetylcholine is found in large quantities. Neurotransmitters are chemicals that pass information between nerve cells. If acetylcholine is depleted, memory disturbances occur. It is like running out of fuel. Drugs such as choline are sometimes administered in the hope of restoring acetylcholine (and therefore memory), but the results of such treatments are uneven—and mild at best. A second important neurochemical change that occurs is slowing of brain metabolism with aging. Metabolism is the burning of sugars to produce energy. This energy is used in part to produce acetylcholine. Research has suggested that drugs such as the ergot alkaloids (Hydergine) improve brain metabolism. This is the only drug approved for use in senile dementia by the U.S. Food and Drug Administration.

Electrophysiological Models

Recently, researchers have observed mental activity by measuring brain waves using the electroencephalogram (EEG). When the body's general metabolism slows, as occurs in aging, so do the brain waves. The degree of slowing seems to parallel the degree of mental impairment. It varies from person to person. There are more individual differences among older people than among the young.

Psychological Models

Information Processing (Stimulus-Response)

The information-processing model is a stimulus-response model in which the stimulus, or input, is sensory material. This material is registered and stored in memory. A second stimulus or cue later leads to the response, or output, of the retrieved memory. In other words, any impression to the brain passes through the senses: We see, hear, taste, smell, or feel as a reflex mechanism. We are constantly stimulated by external stimuli. This is usually an unconscious recording process. By becoming aware of it and by reinforcing *consciously selected* stimuli we are sure to encounter when we wish to remember, we can increase the chances of more accurate recall. The stimulus-response pattern works like this: The brain perceives a stimulus which is recorded in the memory center. A cue, or second stimulus, triggers the recall of that recorded memory.

Depth of Processing, or Elaboration

The more deeply information is processed, the better it is recorded and the easier it is to recall. A thought elaborated at length will stay in memory longer than a shallow, fleeting idea. We must write down a new, raw idea because it is not yet woven into a pattern of thought. It is disconnected and therefore fragile and easily erasable. Making mental connections and organizing material are basic to the depth of processing. Repetition is the common method used to make sure that the information is "in," but this mechanical method is superficial and has only short-term effects unless it is complemented by more complex thought processes which leave more elaborate and deeper marks in our memory files. This explains why children forget so rapidly things they repeat by heart without fully understanding them and relating them to their lives. Commenting, asking questions, looking for meaning, relating, and comparing are the mental operations essential to processing information in depth for long-term retention. Emotional as well as intellectual comments are a must, as you will see in the observation training.

Moreover, it has been found that *mood* influences the depth of processing. We tend to remember something we recorded in a certain mood when we are in the same mood. Memories of long ago often convey strong emotions. Events which we find striking when they occur leave a deeper mark in our memories than do neutral events. Each individual colors the neutral stimuli with his or her emotions and cultural context. As Hamlet said, "There is nothing either good or bad but thinking makes it so." We constantly interpret the world around us and record it through our own filters. This is probably why memories of the same event differ so much from witness to witness. As the psychologist Elizabeth Loftus put it, we actually "construct memories," shaping them as we go. Memory is a creative process, and we could participate in it consciously much more than we do.

Temporal Framework

We live within the frame of time, and so do our memories. Some impressions stay in the mind for a few seconds or minutes, while others remain for months or years. (Herriot once said that culture is what is left when we have forgotten everything.) Indeed, there seems to be a selective process at work, sorting out what needs to be remembered for the short term or the long term. This sorting process can be either unconscious or conscious, since we can reinforce selected stimuli and work on the recording of anything we consider valuable information. A curious mind wants to make constant comments, reinforcing previous memories with new associations. This perpetual sifting of information results in culture: We are what we have integrated in our active memory file. We are what we say, what we think, what we do, and what we eat, and these elements all reflect culture as well as personality. Our manners reveal our culture.

Immediate perceptual memory is memory of immediately previous perceptions. It is seldom impaired since there is no need for deep recording, and recall is brought about as a reflex mechanism. Typing is a good example. We read a word and remember it for as long as it takes to type it (usually less than a second). Then it is forgotten, the next word is imprinted in its place, and so on. It is interesting that people who suffer from amnesia have an adequate immediate memory. Unfortunately, immediate memory is not as useful as long-term memory.

Short-term memory is defined by psychologists as lasting a maximum of 5 seconds. It is a working memory, a mental scratch pad which can hold a maximum of *seven* items. It can act as a reference file from which one can extract more specific information. The seven items can be concepts or ideas which in turn will bring about associations and recall. Only constant repetition can keep short-term memory alive. A good example of short-term memory is dialing a phone number you have just looked up. You have to repeat it to yourself to remember the whole number until you have dialed all of it. These first two types of memory do not involve elaborate mental processes and are therefore superficial and vulnerable to interference. If you are interrupted while typing a sentence or dialing a telephone number you have just looked up, you have to go back and start again.

Long-term memory entails more permanent processing and more complex mental operations, although it can refer to varying lengths of time. Long-term memory requires conscious recording of meaningful information. This is called *semantic encoding*. It implies a search for meaning and context in the new material. Without it, learning would be impossible. All new knowledge is to some extent connected to what we already know; beyond the mechanical repetition of short-term memory, the mind searches for connections and works at interpreting the new in terms of the old. For instance, actors learn their roles by integrating their own emotions, gestures, and intellectual backgrounds into the artificial situation of the part, which they have thoroughly analyzed. It usually takes time, concentration, and deep thinking to make a clear recording of new learning. Some people have a natural gift for efficiently organizing information they remember. They are observant, make associations, use their imaginations, and are receptive to intellectual games. The rest of us may not do these things naturally, but we can learn how and thus improve our memories.

Storage

Plato used the metaphor of a wax tablet to describe the way memories are printed in the mind; depending on the quality of the wax, the printing is good or poor. Thus, to him memory seemed to depend entirely on whether one was blessed at birth with the right equipment. Like everything else in the ancient world, one's fate was determined by the gods, and there was little one could do to improve one's condition. In this perspective memory appears as a gift. Plato did not describe what constitutes a good-quality wax or how all these memories printed on tablets of wax are organized. However, in a world with a strong oral tradition (before printing, people had to rely on their memories to pass on the cultural heritage: stories, songs, historical events), Plato probably took for granted the art of mnemonics (aids to memory), which were then widely used.

In recent years, psychologists have focused on the organizational patterns at work when people store material for future recall. They have found that recall depends on how one organizes one's thinking at the time of recording the information. We now recognize that good organization helps memory. But organizational ability, like concentration, is not inherited. Both are learned and therefore can be taught, practiced, and developed at any age. Research in gerontology has shown that the maxim "You cannot teach an old dog new tricks" is false. For years I have been training people above the age of 55, and they *can* learn new behavior patterns when given more time. What prompted me to write this book was people's satisfaction with the results they obtained.

Understanding how memory works is very important because it demystifies the process. Suddenly it becomes accessible and we realize why we remember and why we forget. Plato's metaphor of the wax tablet is still valid because of its visual quality, but nowadays some psychologists find the computer metaphor more accurate because it stresses the organizational processes in memory work. The two are complementary. I prefer to imagine that all impressions, images, feelings, and thoughts are recorded as printed images; our minds act as cameras in much the same way as the fragile tablet of wax. I visualize those images as being classified with the random efficiency of a computer.

Considering the amount of information that gets into the brain, one cannot help marveling at the wonderful mechanism of memory. For most of us, throughout our lives, memories are rather efficiently stored. Files are organized in a network of associations. Classified in a practical way, according to how often they are used, they are pushed up toward consciousness or down toward the unconscious.

Imagine a system of layers. The upper layer is close to consciousness. It contains the useful, the daily, what is often referred to. (I visualize it blue and clear as the day.) Here, for instance, the active vocabulary is stored: names constantly used, familiar phone numbers, etc. It is a very busy place, with files going in and out all the time. Other layers follow where less immediately necessary information is stored.

The middle layer contains passive material that is less often referred to. Memories are accessible through *recognition,* or with a cue to prompt recall. (I visualize this second layer as rust or earth color, a muted color for a quieter place where rusty memories lie undisturbed.) As one gets older and one's activities decrease, the first layer gets smaller at the expense of the second. Here are stored foreign languages once learned and seldom used. I remember how frustrated I was my first day of teaching a memory course in my native France. Some words kept coming to me in English, and there was no time for translation. Many times I stumbled over terms such as "focus," which is delicate to translate, in spite of having prepared myself. My French, no longer useful to me in the United States, had receded. English had replaced it, especially in the particular area of my work. Knowing that that's the way memory works made me feel better, and I soon stopped blaming myself uselessly. Instead, I waited patiently and confidently for the file to move from the rust area to the blue area, which happened the next day under the stimulation of the new environment and a careful rehearsal of my material in French.

The lower layer touches the realm of the unconscious. (I picture it gray like the unknown.) It is probably the largest layer of all, since one records millions of prints from the day one is born. Psychoanalysts say there is an active process called repression that holds down uncomfortable memories in this gray area. That is why people cannot remember what happened to them in traumatic situations (car accidents, rape, etc.). However, most memories are not repressed; they have been pushed down to this gray zone to let other, more pressing matters move closer to consciousness. As we get older and are less busy with an urgent present, we are more open to associations with the past. When we stop looking forward, we start looking backward. This explains in part why you may remember something that happened 20 years ago better than you remember what you had had this morning for breakfast. (But then, if you ate something unusual, such as caviar, I bet you would remember!)

Memories of long ago just wait like Sleeping Beauty to be awakened by a strong sensation. Remote memories need a prompter to return to consciousness. Most often it is a sensory perception or a mood that triggers a chain of images, words, and sensations, recreating a memory recorded long ago. Recall follows the stimulus-response model explained at the beginning of this chapter.

Examples of involuntary memory abound in life and literature. In *Remembrance of Things Past,* Marcel Proust recalls a time he was drinking tea and dipping a cookie into it. As soon as the wet cookie touched his palate, he felt something extraordinary happening: The present with its problems and weariness had vanished, and a deep joy overwhelmed him. He waited eagerly, trying to understand what had caused it. "Suddenly the memory made its appearance." This was the taste of the cookie his aunt Leonie used to give him when he, as a boy, would come to say good morning in her bedroom. Once replaced into its original context, the sensation triggered a chain of recall, images of the happy world of his childhood: "Combray and its surroundings, everything taking shape and volume sprung out, city and gardens, from my cup of tea."

Notice that Proust waited awhile for the recall mechanism to bring back the chain of memories. He helped by concentrating on the sensation of taste and the joy it triggered. Awareness of the sensation is crucial; it provides the necessary time to allow memories to come back. However, it has to be accompanied by a state of quiet openness. Anxiety will block the circuits and postpone recall. Memory is complex and fragile, like a baby. We learn to handle both with a trial and error strategy, often fearing the worst, but through understanding and familiarity we find that both are manageable!

If you want to remember more, be receptive to your senses and observe the wonderful chain of recall of your memories. You can actively participate in the recording and the recall processes, as you will learn in the following chapters. Awareness not only will help your memory, it will give you a deeper enjoyment of the world around you.

Memory Is Imperfect

Nobody can say whether nature is perfect or imperfect. It requires such a broad perspective that we may never know for sure. We see its flaws, but religion and science tell us that they must have a function in the whole creation. The same is true of memory: The flaw in the mechanism—forgetting—has its purpose, and overall it works for our happiness. Memory works for our present needs. We tend to remember what is essential and what is pleasant and forget the rest, including painful events. Sometimes we forget something important, and this can be tragic. Do we store everything that happens to us, or do we leave things out for better or worse? The mechanism of how we remember and how we forget has been studied in recent years in the hope of understanding how accidents occur and why a witness's testimony can be so unreliable. As Elizabeth Loftus explains it, memories are sorted out and we later recall only what has been processed in long-term memory. Figure 2-1 illustrates how "incoming information enters short-term memory where it can be maintained by rehearsal and successfully transfered to long-term memory, or forgotten." Memories are "elaborated" during this transfer. It is a complex mechanism that involves the whole personality.

New studies suggest that one's memory is continually being altered, transformed, or distorted. Loftus explains why memory can fail us: "This is because we often do not see things

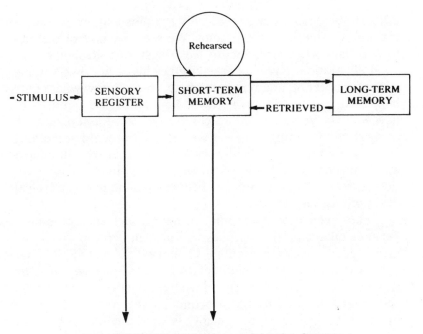

NOT TRANSFERRED to next stage, and therefore forgotten.

Figure 2-1

accurately in the first place. But even if we take in a reasonably accurate picture of some experience, it does not necessarily stay intact in memory. Another force is at work. The memory traces can actually undergo distortion. . . . Even in the most intelligent among us is memory thus malleable.'' Maurice Chevalier's song ''I Remember It Well'' is a spoof on how two lovers remember the past very differently according to their temperaments. He is a romantic; she is down to earth. But was the moon out or not on that special night? We'll never know.

Our minds filter every experience we encounter by means of an unconscious mechanism over which we have little control. Depending on mood, the place and time, cultural bias, and other variables, we choose to remember some things at the expense of others. We may sincerely remember an event in a different way from our friend. This explains why eyewitness's testimony often is of little value: We see only part of the picture, usually what we expect to see. The story of Rashomon is a good illustration. Every character gives his or her own version of the same event, and it proves impossible to know what really happened. However, despite these limitations, we can use our new knowledge and be more careful when we assert that we remember something. Also, if we set out to record something consciously and methodically, chances are that we will have a more objective recollection. People can be trained to pay attention to important clues such as license plate numbers, physical descriptions, and so forth.

Thus, even though memory is not perfect and sometimes depends on unconscious processes, one can improve it through increased conscious awareness. Memory is subjective. It is our own. Let's be content with relative control, as we must be content with the relative control we have over our lives and the way the world goes around. Reconciling the emotional and rational aspects of one's personality is what memory does best. Choose to participate in the process and you will be a winner.

A Useful Metaphor: The Mind as a Camera

Throughout this book I'll be referring to the mind as a camera. Imagine that your mind is a sensitive camera, recording every stimulus it perceives. Most of the time, it is set on automatic focus and you are not conscious of how much effort is necessary to record an accurate image. When memory disturbances occur, your automatic focus is out of order and you must adjust the lens consciously, something you already do when you are absorbed in reading a book you enjoy or in an important task. At such times you select what is worth focusing on according to your goals. You are in control. You are more likely to be creative, since you choose your shots. You check your subject and the angle which most appeals to you. You may even realize that while on automatic focus your mind was more limited. However, it was set to sort out efficiently what was most important to record in a given situation. This is a complex mechanism that works unconsciously as long as you have strong motivation. Work, responsibilities, natural curiosity, and zest for life usually provide sufficient motivation to set the mechanism in motion. Images are sorted out as the situation demands it. You can regain control by shifting to manual, that is, by becoming aware of what it is you want to remember. Then zoom in on it and note as much information as you wish. Conscious recording leaves a better memory trace.

In addition to analyzing the object, think about your mood, your feelings and comment to yourself on this emotional context. You will be helping recall, which is the most delicate step. All this training will develop the curious mind which is asleep in you. Curiosity is the key to attention, and hence to memory.

Quick Review

Memory is a chain made of these essential links:

NEED
or
INTEREST → **MOTIVATION** → **ATTENTION** → **CONCENTRATION** → **ORGANIZATION**

Memory is a complex mental process which we can better understand by looking at it from different perspectives.

A. Physiological

1. Anatomical: The hippocampus, located on the temporal lobes, is the memory center.
2. Neurochemical: Acetylcholine is a chemical that is found in large quantities in the hippocampus; it acts as a neurotransmitter.

3. Electrophysiological: Brain waves (EEG) reflect mental activity.

B. Psychological

1. Information processing (stimulus-response): Selecting a stimulus, becoming aware of it, and reinforcing it help recording and recall.
2. Depth of processing: Awareness of both organizational and emotional responses guarantees better recording. The better the recording, the better the recall.
3. Temporal: There are two kinds of memory. *Short-term memory* is superficial and fragile and needs repetition in order to stay alive more than 5 seconds. *Long-term memory* is deeply set into consciousness. It is reinforced by "semantic encoding," that is, by searching for meaning. It implies complex mental operations.
4. Storage: the layer system

CONSCIOUSNESS

BLUE	Daily useful necessary information (easy recall)	→	ACTIVE
RUST	Less often referred to Recognition memory very good	→	PASSIVE
GREY	Lots of information stored since childhood Needs a prompter to come back to consciousness Stimulus-response involuntary memory	→	LATENT

UNCONSCIOUS

Visualize activity in the blue layer of the present,
passivity in the rust layer of yesterday, and
sleeping beauty in the gray layer of long ago.
This will help you remember the way memories are stored.

5. Memory is imperfect.

Exercises

Exercise 1:   Depth of Processing

Read the following list of 10 words, making the judgment that is suggested along with each word. Read one line at a time, covering the others. Answer yes or no. Then turn the page and write down as many words as you remember.

1. WATER   Would this word be pleasant on a desert island?
2. FLOWER   Does this word have an E in it?
3. TRAIN   Would this word be unpleasant on a desert island?
4. TIRE   Does this word have an E in it?
5. MONTH   Does this word have an E in it?
6. LEG   Would this word be pleasant on a desert island?
7. CHOCOLATE   Does this word have an E in it?
8. PRINCE   Would this word be pleasant on a desert island?
9. CARPET   Does this word have an E in it?
10. KEYS   Would this word be unpleasant on a desert island?

You will have noticed that there are two categories of judgments. Check your list to see which judgment led to better memory. Mark all the words you were asked to associate with pleasant or unpleasant feelings and compare their number with the number of other words you remembered. Now compare the two types of judgment and draw your own conclusion about depth of processing.

Exercise 2:   Immediate Text Review

By now you should have a pretty clear idea of how memory works. *Without rereading,* try your memory. How much of the preceding chapter do you actually remember? Now give your-self a better chance for recall: Review *immediately* what you have just read. Immediate review is the most effective way to remember. Strike while the iron is hot, and you will leave a mark.

Exercise 3:   Attention Test

Most people are not very observant of their surroundings. When you are among friends at home, try this little experiment. Half an hour or so after everyone has been socializing, ask your friends to turn their backs on the person next to them so that they do not see him or her anymore. Explain that you are going to ask a series of questions about this person and that they should write their answers on a piece of paper.

1. Have you noticed the color of his or her outfit? If so, describe it.
2. Is he or she wearing a tie or scarf?
3. Is he or she wearing cologne?
4. What kind of shoes is he or she wearing?
5. Is he or she carrying a bag or purse?
6. Is he or she wearing jewelry? If so, describe it.
7. Describe his or her hair. Color? Texture? Hairstyle?
8. What color are the person's eyes?
9. Is he or she smoking?
10. What is he or she drinking?

NOTE   You can also ask questions about the room people are gathered in. The easiest way to do it is by taking the party to another room or to the garden. You will notice how little observ-ant most people are, but with training anyone can improve.

CHAPTER 3

Memory, Aging, and Mental Attitudes

*"Youth is not entirely a time of life. It is a state
of mind . . . you are as young as your hope, as
old as your despair."*

Anonymous

Memory and Aging

Middle Age

As we get older, we don't necessarily get wiser. We start
losing self-confidence. We are "not so self-assured," to use the
Beatles' words in "Help." Indeed, we begin to feel we need
help as we notice changes in ourselves. The fear of aging plays
tricks on us, distorting our perspective. We feel terrible about
any minor forgetfulness which never used to bother us: misplacing keys twice on a given day, perhaps, or forgetting where
the car is parked. Such things can happen to anyone at any age.
At 20, you don't give it a second thought. At 40, you think,
"What's happening to me? Am I going downhill?" At 60, you
conclude, "I must be getting senile." Your judgment follows
the curve of your anxiety, and deep down you are yearning for
reassurance.

I once helped a young man who was suffering from serious
memory loss as a result of drug overdose. What did he feel most
distressed about forgetting? It was not job-related or personal.
"I can't even remember which switch turns which light in my

entry hall," he confessed. "Neither do I," I caught myself saying. I pointed out that it had never occurred to me to try to remember switches. Most people are satisfied with the trial and error method I call the ape's technique: By touching all the buttons, you eventually hit the right one. One's perspective about memory does not always reflect objective changes. Ask your relatives or close friends about specific changes. Some may be true, but others are imagined. You may have been forgetful all your life without realizing it; you may have relied on others to remember many things. Try to pinpoint your present frustrations, the precise episodes when your memory fails you. Find out if it happened in the past. Ask questions such as "Was I ever good at remembering names of people? Places? Brands? Titles of movies? Books? Shows? Directions? Instructions? Recipes? Appointments? Events? Facts? Trips? Visits? Errands? Messages? The date?" After inquiring about the past, look into the present: "What do I complain about forgetting most nowadays? What did I use to remember easily that I cannot remember now?" Once you have identified an objective change in your memory performance, look for changes in your life which may have affected your motivation. Are you now in a position which allows you to relax without the fear of serious consequences for forgetting something? Do you delegate more responsibilities to others? Do you need to remember this type of information as much as you used to? Do you remember other kinds of information without any trouble? Are you as busy as before, busier, or less busy? Does your present situation deprive you of incentives to pay attention and opportunities to use your memory? When was the last time you had to write a report? Do you often discuss books, articles, or movies in an organized manner?

The answers to these questions should reveal a simple truth: Memory is malleable and practical. When the pressure is off, as is the case when one leaves college or gets a cushier job, the burden is lifted and practice ceases. You may spot a change of pace, a lack of challenges, a mental laziness settling down insidiously, depressive thoughts entering your mind. Is this behavior a normal adaptation to a new reality? Is the potential for memory still there? Memory adapts to the demands of the environment, and most people adjust without trying to live in two realities (past and present) at the same time. When our egos do not adapt to the changes as well as our memories, we perceive a problem. I once met a 38-year-old psychologist who told me about his recent memory loss. "I used to have a fantastic memory: I could remember any reference at professional meetings after having heard it once. Now I must write everything down," he explained. I asked how important remembering these references was to him and to his career. He replied that it was a big asset, setting him apart from others, making him bright and knowledgeable, more likely to be singled out for promotion. At the time of our conversation he had reached his goal; he was his own boss and had no need to impress anyone. The incentive for such a memory feat was removed. Instinctively he had shifted his energies to other kinds of information more relevant to the new situation. He acknowledged that his memory was good in all other contexts. Although he was glad to know he did not have a "real" memory problem, he still yearned for the wonderful feeling he had had while remembering his references. I pointed out that he might want to develop a new memory skill useful in his new job, for example, remembering names and detailed information about his patients. Or he might enjoy his new freedom.

The real psychosocial changes affecting memory should be faced directly, for there is much one can do to help. As Skinner said, "This is an encouraging way to look at aging because more can be done about our environment than about our bodies." You can improve your environment by creating artificial challenges such as finding a friend interested in discussing books, movies, or articles or by learning something new, if only how to improve your memory.

Older Age

One could say that people who age well instinctively know how to adjust to change. All through our lives our bodies change. First the metabolism changes: We need less food as we burn less energy, and if we continue to eat as we did in our teens, we put on weight, adding strain to the heart. Then the brain undergoes subtle changes, but this can be controlled if we keep mentally active. (It is not the number of neurons that count but how we use them. Studies have shown that people use only 10 percent of their brain potential. Thinking strategies make a big difference, especially as we get older. We can learn them at any age.) The environment also changes, and our private lives move on, too. We may end up in another town, far away from friends and relatives; our children leave us to build their own lives; we retire; we sometimes have to face financial hardship and illness; social contacts become scarce; friends die, and are hard to replace.

Darwin showed how animal species survive only if they adjust to changes in the environment. Men and women are no different. The psychologist B. F. Skinner, at age 78, stressed how important it is to accept the changes that come with aging and get organized around them: "A calm acceptance of deficiencies and a more careful observance of good intellectual self-management" may relieve your anxiety. In this chapter you'll learn which changes affect memory and how to deal with them.

Physiological Changes in Normal Aging

Slowing Down

As one gets older, it takes longer to process information and recall it. There is a slight lag in reaction time, which is why people have more difficulty recalling things. Words often escape us, leaving us embarrassed and at a loss. Our reflexes may not be as accurate, our thoughts may be less precise; our bodies and minds change rhythms. Given unlimited time to answer, older people perform just as well on most IQ tests. They have little trouble with recognition tests such as multiple choice, but they have difficulties recalling the answers without a prompter, as in fill-in tests.

If you are beginning to feel your age, take your time and for most tasks you'll do as well as you used to. Ask yourself, "What's the hurry? What difference will a fraction of a second make?" Allow more time when you plan your daily schedule. Avoid rushing. Especially do not get impatient when you are trying to remember something, since the recall mechanism slows down as people get older. Training and strategy can work wonders in compensating for lost energy. Crossword puzzles and chess games have more mature champions than you might expect. I'll bet even video games can be handled at any age with patience and motivation. I tried my hand at Ms. Pacman, and, after many frustrating trials and hours of practice, I noticed that I could play better than many kids. Their reflexes may be slightly faster, but my thinking strategies give me the edge. I found out that nervous tension is my worst enemy. When I manage to relax, I am at my best. (In Chapter 4, "Relaxation," you will learn how to do just that.) Speed is not essential to intellectual function. That is why artists and intellectuals can continue working into their later years. The changes in the mind are less dramatic than those in the body and may be so gradual that they are not perceived as a problem.

Reduced Perception

Perception decreases with age in all people, but to different degrees. Sometimes it leads to a wrong diagnosis: A disoriented patient may look "senile" yet may just have cataracts. You may be blaming your memory unjustly. If you have not heard or seen something, there is no memory trace to be found. The senses are the gateway to brain function, hence to memory. Find out whether you have any deficits (hearing, sight, taste, smell, or touch) and take the necessary steps to correct them. Sit closer to the screen or closer to people; ask them to repeat. Turn your ear toward the speaker's mouth. Use technical aids whenever possible: corrective glasses, a magnifying glass, or a hearing aid, for instance. Above all, pay more attention than usual, using the methods you will learn in this book. By using and developing all your senses, you can compensate for your weaker ones, and, in so doing, you will enrich your life and your memory.

Shorter Attention Span

Attention span also decreases with age, and older people cannot work efficiently for long periods of time. If you find that you tire more easily, accept that fact. Take pauses, naps, or walks whenever your concentration dwindles. Invigorate your brain with fresh air and exercise. Change activities. Divide your task into smaller units of time. Instead of reading for 1 hour, take a break after a half hour (use a bookmark to quickly find your page), get up, and move around. If you have a back problem, sit in a different chair. Avoid overly soft cushions, as they induce sleep. Also be sure the light is adequate: You should not be straining. The right amount of comfort is necessary to maintain attention.

Sensitivity to Interference

Yes, people are more easily distracted as they get older, and interferences can really jolt the memory. Do not feel bad if you forget what you were doing before you were interrupted. Just go back to where you were or walk through the house looking around: You'll soon find a visual cue to bring you back so that you can pick up where you left off. For important tasks such as writing checks, get organized so that you will not be disturbed. Get into the habit of disregarding the phone the first few times it rings: It will give you time to wrap up what you were doing and plant a cue for when you come back. End the tyranny of the phone! Tell your friends and relatives to let it ring six times. Also, write down important thoughts or notes of what you were doing when interrupted. If you want to listen better, look at a neutral spot on the floor: It will minimize distractions. When you read or study, turn off the TV or radio and choose a quiet place with no visual stimulation, such as pictures, photographs, and windows. You'll be helping your concentration.

Difficulty Performing Several Tasks at the Same Time

As a consequence of being highly sensitive to interference, older people find it more difficult to do several things at the same time. For example, don't talk while writing a check, signing a document, or driving and looking for directions. Focus on one task at a time, and you will do well on each one. If your personality prompts you to do many things at the same time, you may be a "type A"; it will be harder but not impossible to stop that tendency. It may be a blessing in disguise that nature slows people down. This kind of activity (called polymorphic activity) causes not only memory problems but also heart disease through the stress it puts on your system. As you get older, do you need so much pressure? Consider your life situation and see if you deserve a break. Select an order of priorities and do one thing at a time. You will feel great!

Memory Capacity

Memory function decreases by 20 to 40 percent with age. There are wide individual differences in aging, some of which are genetic. Possibly the brain is more crowded by obsessive, depressing thoughts and anxiety. If so, getting rid of them should restore adequate memory capacity. Freeing the mind to think more efficiently is the first goal of memory training.

Lack of Spontaneous Organization

It becomes increasingly difficult to think in an organized manner. Partly it may be lack of practice when one's activities decrease, but people also tend to rehearse old patterns, leaving little room for new ones. We seem less willing to experiment with new ideas. Skinner suggests that creative people reaching old age should "learn a new intellectual style" and work on new subjects rather than rehash the same ones. Anybody can learn new thinking strategies, thus compensating for the decrease in spontaneous organization. It is just one more example of shifting from automatic to manual.

Drugs

If you are taking any drugs, check with your doctor about side effects. Some medications may make you drowsy or mentally scattered and interfere with memory by reducing attention and slowing your mental function.

Illness and Senility

One of the biggest fears as one gets old is the fear of senility. Now and again you hear people making remarks such as "I misplaced my checkbook twice today, I must be getting senile." Avoid the word "senile"; it is disparaging and widely misused. Only 12 percent of the population over age 65 suffers from senile dementia, a disease characterized by severe memory loss, disorientation, and often paranoid behavior. It strikes both sexes equally, but more women are affected because they live longer. Most people with the disease are in their midseventies or mideighties. If you are worried about your memory, chances are that you do not have this disease. Senile people are *not* aware of being forgetful, and they often resent having it pointed it out to them.

The other two mental illnesses affecting memory are Alzheimer's disease and Korsakoff's syndrome. Alzheimer's disease is a precocious form of senile dementia that strikes people in the prime of life, sometimes as early as the forties. Now the term is used for all ages and is a synonym for senile dementia. (The medical term is "senile dementia of the Alzheimer's type.") It is associated with the depletion of a chemical in the brain essential to memory function. This substance, called acetylcholine, is lost in great quantities and cannot be replaced. There is research going on, but the ultimate cure has not been discovered to this day. This is irreversible brain damage similar to what occurs in Korsakoff's syndrome, which is caused by alcoholism. For these unfortunate patients the care is often limited to family support groups and practical help in coping with the affliction. However, these are *abnormal* conditions which have nothing to do with normal aging.

We have seen which physiological changes are inevitable in normal aging and which are accidental (illnesses). If you are still concerned about your degree of forgetfulness, consult a neurologist or psychiatrist. People with brain damage cannot function in everyday life. The onset of the mental illnesses described in the preceding paragraphs is slow and unpredictable. It often goes undetected until people become dependent on others. Usually the family rather than the patient notices the memory gaps. By contrast, normal people with memory complaints tell me about all the things they have forgotten in the past week. The funny thing is that they remember every instance accurately. If for some unfortunate patients the future still looks grim, they are a small minority. As you can see, for most people there is hope. We can deal with the normal physiological changes. However, memory problems also stem from psychosocial changes which are reversible in many cases.

Psychosocial Changes in Later Life

Retirement

A change of pace or a reduction of activities often produces memory problems. With fewer "reinforcements" from the environment, we don't have the incentive to pay as much attention as we did in the past. Let's face it, we don't have as much to lose if we don't keep on our toes. It is human to let go when the pressure is off. The problem is that responsibilities give us the incentive to select, focus, and organize. Without them we are often at a loss. *Activity* is the key to mental as well as physical function. If we stop exercising our bodies, our joints freeze. If we stop using our brains, our minds go to pot. The challenge lies in finding new activities and defining new goals with obvious rewards.

Hobbies are most important once one retires, because they often become the main activity in one's life. We must find some meaningful and pleasurable activity to fill our minds and our days. Use the skills you have to enrich the lives of those around you. Many people choose this time in life to make some dreams come true. Although few people can afford a cruise around the world, everyone can learn to relax and enjoy oneself. The important thing is to allow yourself to be satisfied with a new lifestyle that may be very different from the work ethic you followed all your life. As Skinner points out, "It may be necessary in old age to acquire new ways of thinking." Retirement may be a time for reflection. May I suggest that you reconsider the idea of usefulness: Is it essential to happiness?

Leisure can be rewarding or destructive. You may feel guilty with so much leisure on your hands since society, and often one's religion, praises the work ethic. Tell yourself you deserve to relax and take it easy. Then restructure your life around what you most enjoy doing: Keep your mind busy and continue using your skills. You may want to explore adult education programs in your community. You may decide to teach (sharing knowledge is most rewarding) or learn about an interesting subject. Now is your chance to do woodwork or learn Spanish. The incentive may be a trip to Mexico or meeting people with common interests. Above all, challenge your mind and share your thoughts with curious-minded people: We usually need an audience of at least one person to perform. Choose a specific goal such as learning about flowers, birds, or sailing and keep jogging your memory.

Living Alone

It may be difficult to live alone if you have spent most of your life living with someone. Relationships are binding because they create mutual dependency. You may have relied on your partner to remember many things, and now you are suddenly burdened by so many details that you think you cannot handle it. It takes time to rebuild your life, especially during the grieving period after the loss of a loved one. Losing a spouse is traumatic, and it causes many disturbances. Someone once said that grief carries along its own anesthetic: We feel numb, unable to grasp the new reality without the loved one. This numbness protects us from pain we cannot bear, but it also makes it impossible to control our attention.

Structure your life so that you continue to take care of your basic needs. Above all, keep your physical health. Remember that sound bodies build strong minds. Following a routine helps compensate for lack of motivation: It breaks the round of self-defeating questions such as "Who cares if I take a shower?" Get up upon awakening, fix yourself breakfast, go out for errands, and make sure you eat one full meal a day. For some people this will seem impossible. It is not. Anyone can learn to cook simple, nutritious meals. Cooking classes for singles are offered in many community centers. Avoid nibbling on junk food: It curbs the appetite without providing the nutrients your body needs. Nutrition and alertness are related, and so are diet and longevity.

You can help your mind adjust to changes. There are ways to chase the blues. Your moods can control you, or you can learn to control them when you are unhappy. All you need to do is find some sensory stimulation such as nature or music. Diversion works wonders. Create your own. Instead of feeling sorry for yourself, *do something:* Read, watch a movie, or take a walk in a park and enjoy the trees, the flowers, the birds. Keep your mind busy observing the beauty which surrounds you. Enjoy the sun, the fresh air, the rain, the wind. When you do that, you are combining physical exercise with relaxation. Or turn to music: It creates moods and can dissipate gloomy thoughts provided that you choose the right kind of music. Whether you prefer jazz, folk music, rock, or classical, select uplifting pieces. I find baroque music (Mozart, Handel, Vivaldi, Bach, Pachelbel) especially cheerful and soothing; it reflects an ideal of serenity the happy few enjoyed at that time. Nineteenth-century music is also gay but not as peaceful to me. The music of the romantics (Chopin, Beethoven, Schubert, Schumann, Wagner, Mendelssohn, Liszt) expresses this mixture of nostalgia for the past and passion for an unknown future. It is full of strong emotions, a music of extremes—extreme joy or extreme sadness—and it touches the soul at an emotional level much more than the even-keeled tones of the baroque composers. Whichever music you choose to listen to will change your mood and divert your thoughts. The new mood will bring you more than a change. It will trigger memories which will add to your well-being. Time passes, but we capture it with our memories. We can learn to recapture them when we want. It is an invaluable skill, especially for those who are alone. Happy memories provide entertainment. Research has revealed that mood is a powerful enhancer of memories. Create the mood you like and you will reawaken memories that were recorded in the same mood.

Losses

The more one has, the more one stands to lose. People experience many losses in later life: They lose spouses, friends, and relatives but also physical capacities and status. Most older people are on reduced incomes, and so they lose much of their purchasing power. They also lose reinforcement for whatever it is they do. Upon retiring, the social role, the on-the-job pride, the authority, the power, and the prestige suddenly vanish. With the loss of responsibilities comes a lack of concrete rewards for action. Nobody seems to care anymore one way or the other. All these losses lead to depression, which is the number one cause of memory problems as people get older. Depression is the result of a combination of changes in metabolism and in a person's life. A great deal of biochemical evidence shows that as we get older, we lose biogenic amines, and therefore we are more vulnerable to depression. (An excess of biogenic amines causes euphoria.) But losses also play a major role in the onset of depression. We see ourselves alone, without a future. The present is too empty and painful to be dwelt on, so we start living in the past. As we disregard the present, we stop caring for anything around us, including ourselves. Losses can lead to neglect, malnutrition, and severe depression, and they always trigger memory problems.

Grieving: If you have recently lost a loved one, accept the grieving process. Attention deficits are normal in this condition.

Be patient with yourself, knowing that your memory troubles are only temporary. Allow yourself to express sorrow; bottling it up will only delay recovery. Open up to a sympathetic friend or look for "grief therapy" groups in your community. Sharing experiences has proved to be therapeutic. Do not suffer alone when you can get help. Get out of the house, and you will find diversions. Force yourself to get involved in something. A game of cards or a visit to the local library or community center is better than self-pity and loneliness. You need contacts, activities to rebuild your present. You need stimulation so that your mental functions continue working. The longer you stay inactive, the worse your memory is going to get. Severe depression can be treated with medications, so see your doctor if you feel that these suggestions are not sufficient.

Mental Attitudes

Depression and negative attitudes go hand in hand. Our outlook on life determines how we experience it. As the French philosopher Jean Marie Guyau said, "The future is not what is coming to meet us, but what we are moving forward to meet." This quotation hits the crystal ball of all fortune-tellers by revealing a simple truth: We actually determine our own future by the way we live our present. If we want to be content with our future life, we must be more aware of what we think and do now and of the consequences of our actions and reactions. We may be sabotaging ourselves without knowing it and perhaps looking for someone or something to blame for our shortcomings. Underlying such behavior are conscious and unconscious attitudes we have derived from our education and social environment. Our mental attitudes determine the course of action we will take. And action, or lack of it, will determine our future failure or success.

Perhaps the hottest ingredient of success is the belief that it may happen, that it is possible. This positive attitude gives one the motivation to persevere and do what it takes to get where one wants to go. Without faith in gold, the west might not have been conquered. Pioneering was just too tough for most people.

True, not everyone found gold, but many found other riches and a new territory in which to build a new world. Their basic hope was rewarded because they believed in it enough to follow through with action. Skill, knowledge, talent, and opportunity do make a difference, but they all depend on a positive frame of mind. You will never learn a skill or grasp an opportunity if you are convinced it will not do any good. You must disregard the odds if you are to attempt the ascent. By not attempting, you kill the possibility of success. Some behavioral therapists suggest that pretending you can make it may remove the block to action which guarantees failure. In other words, by acting like a success, you may become one. Sports are a good example. Winning teams and athletes project themselves as winners; in fact, the East German teams use positive visualization in their training. A positive attitude works wonders.

Since you are reading this book, you must be dissatisfied with your memory. You should realize right now that unless you *expect* an improvement, you are not going to make the effort necessary for it to happen. I strongly believe that anyone can improve his or her memory with some guidance and the right mental attitude. But be realistic: Expect improvement, not perfection. The *Oxford English Dictionary* defines "attitudes of mind" as "settled mode of thinking," in other words, a *fixed* way of thinking that expresses our assumptions, beliefs, expectations, and prejudices. These ways of thinking become part of our lives, and so we do not question them anymore: They are us. That is why they are sometimes difficult to identify and always hard to change. Our *conscious* attitudes are those with which we feel comfortable. We acknowledge them as parts of our personalities, for better or worse: "That's the way I am." But there are many *unconscious* attitudes of which we are not aware. They make us do things we often do not understand even when someone points them out to us. Psychiatrists say we repress them because deep down we feel bad about them. For instance, you may have decided that you have a poor memory as an excuse for not trying to remember many things you do not care about. Rebelling against the system strengthens this attitude. Prejudices are often unconscious attitudes: You may have met people who express racist ideas and act accordingly while thinking and saying they are not racist.

Many attitudes interfere with memory. We shall identify those negative attitudes, analyze them, and hopefully replace them with positive ones. Attitudes express themselves in thoughts, speech, and actions. We may not consciously know how often we sabotage our efforts to remember something. For instance, the old saying "You cannot teach an old dog new tricks" may be enough to discourage you from learning anything at any age you consider old. I have heard people say it is impossible to learn foreign languages after the age of 30, learn a new sport when you retire, and so forth. The facts prove otherwise, but if you think it is impossible to learn after age 30, you will never try and therefore will never learn, although the capacity for learning may be there. (This explains certain effects of witchcraft as well as the placebo effect in medical research: If you believe that something false is true, your belief may make it come true.)

It is important to know if you are unconsciously doing something against your desire to improve your memory. You can correct a negative attitude and replace it with a positive one that will bring about the change you expect. You don't have to be clinically depressed to suffer from depressive attitudes. Such attitudes can affect your memory and thought processes in two important ways. First, they can cause a slowing down and a feeling of confusion resulting from a lack of concentration. When we are depressed or anxious, our minds are occupied only with our sadness and problems. It is like an obsession that disconnects us from the outside reality. The world loses its grip on us; we stop listening, looking, and often feeling what is not related to our worries. We become self-centered and forget many things. Second, depressive and other negative attitudes can inhibit and sabotage your attempts to remember something by reinforcing the behaviors that keep you away from action. Thoughts such as "I've got a mind like a sieve," "I'm too old to try," and "I'll be making a fool of myself" prevent you from doing anything for your memory. They also destroy self-esteem.

Unfortunately, this "negative emotionality" is a prominent personality trait in many people, and such individuals suffer more from age than others. In her book *Goddesses in Every-woman,* Jean Shinoda Bolen suggests that women with an independent core fare better during the years of widowhood but that any woman can develop different qualities at different periods of her life. Independence seems to be a positive trait when fewer people depend on you. Therefore, middle age is a good time to start cultivating this quality.

The exercises in this chapter will allow you to identify the negative attitudes you need to eliminate and help you substitute positive ones. The major depressive attitudes are *hopelessness, helplessness,* and *worthlessness.* Here are a few examples of what you may be telling yourself.

1. "Of course I don't remember—I'm getting older." The core of this attitude is hopelessness. Unfortunately, it is not only an individual attitude but a cultural expectation shared by many people in our society. Scientific studies show that in many cases decline in intellectual function and memory in the aged does not have to be permanent. It's the depressive attitude that makes this real for many people. Instead, say to yourself, "My memory may have declined, but I can work to make what I have more efficient and useful to me."

2. "I don't need my memory anymore," or the variant, "I won't have to remember anything at the old folks home." This attitude of worthlessness is also both an individual attitude and a cultural expectation. Retirement, with its loss of intellectual and social stimulation from the job and the sudden isolation and lack of social status, gives a strong message of worthlessness to older people. The facts are that less than 15 percent of the population over age 65 is in any kind of institution. Instead, say to yourself, "I may be over 55, but I want to keep sharp. I owe it to myself."

3. "I can't improve my memory; it's gone." The core of this attitude is helplessness. Age-related decline *can* be reversed. In most psychological research the issue has been found to be not whether memory will improve but how much. Instead, say to yourself, "My memory isn't what I want it to be, but it's possible, with a little help and some method, for me to improve it."

4. "My memory is awful. I can't remember the World Series pitch by pitch." This attitude, commonly called perfectionism, is related to depression by its implication that nothing short of perfection is worthwhile. A more realistic attitude might be "I may not remember everything I used to, but I make sure to remember what's important."

5. "When I am done with this book, I should be able to memorize the Sunday paper." Like perfectionism, sky-high expectations are a variant of hopelessness because they are unrealistic. The unspoken part is "If this treatment does not work like magic, it is a failure and so am I." Instead, say, "I'll make a point to remember what interests me."

6. "I should be doing better. This is too much work," "This takes too much time," or "I didn't realize I had to practice." By means of such rationalizations we can quit before we get a chance to see a change. Magic is instant gratification of desire, while any real-world treatment takes time. You must be patient. Cognitive training takes practice and goodwill effort, but the effort can be pleasant, even fun. Think of these exercises as a game and you'll enjoy them. A more realistic attitude might be "Memory is a skill that I can practice and improve."

Finally, it is important to realize that all these changes affect your memory. With this information in hand, you can raise your expectations. Accepting a new reality and making some adjustments are the first steps toward improving your memory. The situation has to improve first, and then you will be more interested in the outside world and your attention will be better. You'll be able to concentrate and learn what pays off to ensure good recording and good recall. With memory techniques you will compensate for the inevitable changes that come with age.

Quick Review

The changes that occur with aging and affect memory are as follows.

A. Physiological changes in normal aging
  1. Slowing down, tiring more easily
  2. Reduced perception
  3. Shorter attention span
  4. Greater sensitivity to interference
  5. Slightly reduced memory capacity
  6. Lack of spontaneous organization
  7. Reduced ability to do several things at once
  Other physiological changes are due to drugs or illnesses. Check these with your doctor if you are worried.

B. Psychosocial and emotional changes in normal aging
  1. Midlife changes
  2. Retirement
  3. Living alone
  4. Losses
  5. Depression
  6. Mental attitudes

We have pinpointed the areas to work on to improve memory in one's later years. Reduced attention combined with reduced organizational ability weaken our memories, but we can improve both and increase the chances of recall.

Exercises

Exercise 1: Negative Attitudes Related to Memory

Rewrite the following from the standpoint of a positive attitude.

1. It's too much effort analyzing things, searching for associations. I would rather forget.
2. I just cannot relax. My thoughts are scattered, and I cannot concentrate. I'm just too anxious.
3. I cannot pause and make sure I finish what I am doing before starting on something else. My case is hopeless.
4. I did not understand what she said, but I don't dare ask her to repeat it.
5. I cannot read without a magnifying glass, and my glasses are too weak. It's too much effort. It's not worth it.
6. I used to love movies; now I don't go anymore because I get drowsy and cannot follow the plot when I wake up.

Exercise 2:   Attitudes in Readings

1. Read the following poems about aging and identify negative attitudes and positive ones.
2. Rephrase the negative poems in your own positive words.

The Old Men Admiring Themselves in the Water

I heard the old, old men say,
"Everything alters,
And one by one we drop away."
They had hands like claws, and their knees
Were twisted like the old thorn-trees
By the waters.
I heard the old, old men say,
"All that's beautiful drifts away
Like the waters."

W.B. Yeats

To Satch

Sometimes I feel like I will NEVER stop
Just go on forever

Till one fine mornin'
I'm gonna reach up and grab me a handfulla stars
Swing out my long lean leg
And whip three hot strikes burnin' down the heavens
And look over at God and say,
How About That!

Samuel Allen

Untitled

The cherry tree blossomed. Black was my hair.
I laughed and danced with girls young and fair.
The cherry tree blossomed. Gray was my hair.
But the blossoms were youthful everywhere.
The cherry tree is still a thing of delight,
While a laughing god turned my hair to white.

Tomonori (9–10 century)

When You Are Old

When you are old and gray and full of sleep,
And nodding by the fire, take down this book,
And slowly read, and dream of the soft look
Your eyes had once, and of their shadows deep.

How many loved your moments of glad grace,
And loved your beauty with love false or true;
But one man loved the pilgrim soul in you,
And loved the sorrows of your changing face.

And bending down beside the glowing bars
Murmur, a little sadly, how love fled
And paced upon the mountains overhead
And hid his face amid a crowd of stars.

W.B. Yeats

Exercise 3:   Awareness

Think about any changes that have recently occurred in your life. They can include apparently small things as well as major events. For instance, have you discovered a new shop, made a new acquaintance, changed your routine? Write down the changes and try to express how you feel about them. Go a step further and analyze whether they have produced other changes. Ask yourself how it all affects you.

You will become aware of changes that modify your lifestyle, sometimes creating new habits which you may or may not want. For example, a friend noticed her figure changing, a few dimples of fat settling around her hips. Rather than accept her first thought, "I'm getting older," she started looking for changes in her food habits. She noticed a major one: A few months before, she had discovered a bread she found wonderful. She had to admit that never before had she indulged in so much bread and butter. Also, she had not been exercising, because in bad winter weather she took her car rather than walk. Awareness made her understand the change and gave her the opportunity to control how much she ate as well as get some needed exercise.

Next, look for changes which may affect your memory. For instance, you have recently been preoccupied by health or family or professional problems, and your attention span is nonexistent. Identify examples of memory lapses (e.g., you forgot to buy bread or pick up a friend or return a phone call). Think of something you could do to help your memory during this time of stress. (You could use visual reminders, such as sticker notes strategically placed where you cannot miss them.)

CHAPTER 4

Relaxation

*"When we are unable to find tranquility within
ourselves, it is useless to seek it elsewhere."*

La Rochefoucauld (*Maximes*)

Problems of attention lie at the core of memory disturbances. Without attention, nothing can be recorded in our
minds, and hence nothing can be recalled. Lack of attention can
result from different causes, but anxiety is the most common.
When one is anxious, one is preoccupied with anxiety. When
people fear they will not be able to remember something, they
waste time and energy worrying instead of doing what has to be
done to fix a memory: concentrating on what is to be remembered.

The fear of forgetting is one of the strongest blocks to memory. The mind becomes obsessed by it, partially because of
previous failures. It exaggerates the consequences of memory
lapses and prompts us to quit trying, and the self-fulfilling
prophecy comes true. Learning to downplay failures helps control anxiety. As B. F. Skinner suggests: "Some help may come
from making such situations as free from aversive consequences as possible. Graceful ways of explaining your failure
may help. Appeal to your age." Or just accept the margin of
error which is part of the memory process. Learning to deal
with these episodes is important, because it will reduce their
frequency.

Paying attention is being aware, aware of what is going on
within ourselves as well as around us. As we become conscious

of our inner turmoil, we can start doing something about it. But there is a paradox in memory. The harder one tries to force a recollection, the more elusive it becomes. The reason, clearly, is an interference with attention. If asked the name of a flower growing in your garden, you may be surprised and feel under pressure to respond immediately. Failure to remember will then bring about tension and anxiety, making it all the more difficult, perhaps almost impossible, for you to deliver a satisfactory answer. It is important to eliminate this anxiety, because once you are relieved of it, the channels of memory will open and you will remember more easily.

Learn to react positively in the face of blatant forgetfulness. If indeed you cannot recall something when and where you want to, try not to feel guilty. Do not berate yourself and make a mountain out of a molehill. This small episode does not prove that you are losing your memory and going downhill. Put the incident in perspective and acknowledge the fact that it has happened to you before (as it happens to everyone), although you never paid much attention to it (for one thing, you were probably too busy to dwell on it). Tell yourself, "It's normal to forget sometimes. It will come back later." The sooner your anxiety level drops, the sooner memories will spring back. When you are more confident, you are more relaxed. You can also improve your memory by redirecting your thoughts away from your anxiety: Thinking about how to perform a task dissolves the tension by keeping your mind busy with practical steps. For example, instead of feeling bad because you cannot remember how to change a tire, analyze the parts and think about how you can take it apart and put it back together. You will remember how to do it as soon as your mind is off your anxieties and on your task.

Here is what Professor Aitken, a man much studied by psychologists for his extraordinary memory, says about relaxation: "I discovered that the further I proceeded, the more I needed relaxation, not concentration as ordinarily understood. At first one might have to concentrate, but as soon as possible one should *relax*. Very few people do that. Unfortunately it is not taught at school, where knowledge is acquired by rote."

In this chapter we are going to learn how to relax in order to increase attention. Concentration is often confused with tension. In fact, it is quite the opposite: In order to concentrate, we must be relaxed and open to observation. The following methods will allow you to unwind and relax. You will discover how effortless remembering can be once you free yourself of interference.

You will learn the classic relaxation technique of *progressive muscle relaxation*. People are rarely taught how to relax, yet it is an important and learnable ability. The technique is completely safe and involves no stress or strain as you might expect in some forms of yoga. We shall just work on tension in the hands, arms, legs, and face. You will not be asked to do anything involving your back or neck. The following pages include an outline of the procedure that constitutes the exercises in this chapter. After you have learned the relaxation method, we shall continue with anxiety-reduction exercises.

Think of these relaxation exercises as mental hygiene. Practice progressive muscle relaxation routinely every day in the morning and in the evening, plus whenever you feel tense or restless. Get into the habit of doing the deep-breathing exercises before you undertake any task which requires your attention. They will help you relax and release excess tension, which interferes with concentration. Then you will be free to record your memories with more self-control.

Progressive Muscle Relaxation

Do this exercise at home or in a closed room. It is important to be alone in a quiet place when you are trying to relax. Avoid being disturbed or interrupted. The purpose of this relaxation exercise is to prove that when your muscles are relaxed, so are you. Once muscular tension is gone, you should feel free from inner tension. Releasing muscular tension is the easiest way to relax. This is why one feels relaxed after exercising.

1. Sit down in a comfortable chair with your legs un-
   crossed and your feet touching the floor. Loosen any
   tight clothing and let your limbs rest limp.

2. Point your toes, tensing the muscles in your feet and
   legs. Hold 10 seconds, then relax. When I tell you to
   relax after tensing and holding, I mean drop. Let your
   limbs fall by their own weight. This is a sudden movement corresponding to a release of tension. It is essential to let go completely after tensing the muscles. Be
   aware of it. You should feel a warm sensation: the blood
   rushing through your muscles. Enjoy this sensation and
   breathe normally for about 20 seconds before tensing
   the next set of muscles.

3. Flex your toes, keeping your heels on the floor for support, and again tense the muscles in your feet and legs.
   Hold for 10 seconds and then relax for 20 seconds. In
   steps 2 and 3 you should feel the muscles of your feet
   and legs tense and warm up. Enjoy the wonderful feeling of relaxation that follows tension.

4. Lift your legs up parallel to the floor, pointing your toes
   as in step 2. Hold for 10 seconds and then relax. Now
   your feet, legs, and thighs should feel nice and warm.

5. Repeat step 4, adding a new set of muscles: the but-
   tocks. Hold for 10 seconds and then relax. We have
   now worked with the lower half of the body. Next we
   shall add the muscles of the upper part.

6. Lift your arms horizontally (parallel to the floor).
   Clench your fists and tense your whole arm. Hold for 10
   seconds and then relax. Repeat with spread-out hands
   and wide-open fingers. Hold for 10 seconds and then
   relax.

7. Make an O with your mouth stretched forward and open
   your eyes wide in a comic expression of surprise. Avoid
   frowning. Hold for 10 seconds and then relax. Your face
   and neck muscles will thank you for it. (Try this while
   waiting at a red light.)

8. Smile as hard as you can. Hold for 10 seconds and then relax. See, you have reached the end of the exercise with a smile!

Muscle Relaxation through Visualization

This exercise is a yoga technique used to put both body and mind in a state of total relaxation after you have exercised the muscles. Therefore, it is a good idea to do it after the progressive muscle relaxation exercise. It is an easy way to check the degree of relaxation you have achieved.

1. Lie on your back on a comfortable surface, such as a carpet or a bed, or sit in a high-back armchair or couch.

2. Close your eyes and visualize an image that evokes peace and quiet to you—the seashore, perhaps, or a lake with small rustling waves—or picture yourself floating gently on an air mattress in a quiet pool, dozing in a boat rocking gently on a calm lake, or soaking up the sun on a sandy beach. Form a clear picture in your mind.

3. Then, starting with the feet and progressing slowly to the head, command each set of muscles to relax. Wait 1 second between commands. Become aware of the remaining tension as this exercise helps you eliminate it. Relax each part of your body in order as you whisper mentally in a monotone:

Relax your feet,
Relax your toes,
Relax your legs,
Relax your knees,
Relax your thighs,
Relax your stomach,
Relax your chest,

Relax your arms,
Relax your hands,
Relax your fingers,
Relax your neck,
Relax your face,
Relax your jaws,
Relax your mouth,
Relax your tongue,
Relax your eyes,
Relax your eyelids,
Relax your eyebrows,
Relax your forehead,
Relax your cheeks,
Relax completely.

Let go of all tension. Listen to your breathing: It should be shallow and regular. Now you are in harmony. Luxuriate in the feeling of well-being which you are experiencing. Enjoy this moment of perfect relaxation.

Note that you can do this exercise any time, any place, whenever you feel tense. It is wonderful to know that through visualization and suggestion you can get rid of the discomfort which tension brings. Some people carry tension in their shoulders, others in their faces, frowning or squinting without being aware of it. This technique helps identify stress and relieve it.

Deep Breathing and Visualization: The Waves

You can achieve a wonderful state of relaxation by concentrating on your breathing. Breathe deeply, focusing on the air coming in and out of your nostrils. Maintain a slow, regular pace.

1. Sit comfortably without tensing your muscles. Do not cross your arms, legs, or hands. Let your limbs rest limp.

2. Inhale deeply and gradually *through your nose* until your lungs are full.

3. Exhale slowly, also *through your nose,* until all the air is out. Try to pace yourself; do not collapse immediately.

4. Start a new cycle, listening to your breath rushing in and slowly going out. Listen carefully to the rhythm of your breath. Notice how it sounds like waves crashing gently ashore (exhalation), only to be reborn in the next phase (inhalation) as they build up strength rolling along sand and pebbles toward the sea. Visualize the movement of the waves, their sound, the smell of the sea, the feel of a fresh morning breeze—enjoy! This should be a very soothing image. Focus on it throughout the exercise. You may not want to come out of it.

NOTE   All breathing exercises aimed at total relaxation should be done with the mouth closed. As one yogi said, "The mouth is made for kissing and eating only." This may sound dogmatic, but keep in mind that yogis do not run or do aerobic exercises. True, when your body is in movement, you must breathe with your mouth open. Not so when you are at rest and want to relax. If you have a cold and your nose is stuffed, postpone this exercise.

Do this exercise as often as you can but especially when you feel tense, uptight, under pressure, or angry and of course when you just cannot remember something. Focus on the smooth rhythm of the waves. No need to overfill your lungs or push to expel the air: Easy does it! This is the most effective method I know to relieve tension on the spot and clear the way for concentration.

Deep-Breathing Relaxation: The Balloon

The following exercise is a variant of "The Waves." As you switch images, you change emphasis from a smooth rhythm to a light, floating feeling. Here you will keep the air in your lungs a little longer.

1. Sit in a comfortable position with your muscles limp.
2. Close your eyes for better concentration.
3. Inhale deeply through your nose to a count of 4.
4. Hold your breath for a count of 4 *without forcing or pushing* on your stomach muscles. Do not block your breathing; doing so will make you tense. Since holding is often associated with tension, say mentally, "Float, gently, in suspension." This will help you feel detached, as if in a state of suspension. If you still find you must strain in order to hold your breath, skip this step and go on to the next.
5. Exhale slowly through your nose for a count of 8.
6. Inhale deeply again for a new cycle of deep-breathing relaxation.

NOTE It is helpful to visualize your lungs as an inflated balloon floating gently in the air and then deflating little by little, slowly, until completely empty. Choose a colored balloon of the sort that small children like.

Wait until you resume normal, shallow breathing before starting a new cycle. Above all, do not rush. You want to develop a smooth rhythm, inhaling gradually, floating gently, and exhaling slowly.

Try doing this exercise five times in a row, three times a day. Practice it before you undertake any task which requires all your attention. Deep-breathing relaxation can be done anywhere and at any time. Whenever you feel tense, breathe deeply and rhythmically, and you will feel relieved. Do not rush or force, and do not hyperventilate. If you tend to hyperventilate, skip this exercise and concentrate on the waves.

Reducing Anxiety by Anticipation

Since anxiety destroys attention and memory, it is very important to prevent such mental interruptions. An actor forgetting his lines, a speaker forgetting her speech, and a student forgetting the material the examiner asks about all are affected by anxious interferences. Each knows the material, but the channels of memory are cluttered by anxiety. Something (whether exterior or interior) triggers a feeling of panic: "What if I can't go on?" "What if I forget my demonstration?" "What if I forget my part and everyone laughs at me?" "What if they do not buy it?" "This person has a skeptical look on her face; I'm failing to convince." All these questions should be predictable. You can deal with them *before* you are put on the spot.

Imagine the Worst

Anticipating an event in a negative way brings anxiety, but you can also use anticipation to cope better with reality. As the saying goes, forewarned is forearmed. Imagine and visualize yourself in the dreaded situation. Rehearse your part in your mind, anticipate your fear, ride with it, intensify it, but stop before you feel uncomfortable. Now concentrate on your fear. Identify it and experience it in your mind. Imagine your physical reactions: sweating, blushing, raising your voice or letting it fade away. By comparison, the real event will appear less threatening. Also, test the rational grounds that may be the source of your insecurity: Do you really know the material? Are you prepared to answer any question? Analyze the reasons for your fear. Review the event in your mind and see if there is any cause for so much anxiety. If there is, this is the time to prepare yourself so that you will be more secure as you speak in public. If, however, you find no real cause for anxiety, you will be reassured and have confidence in yourself.

NOTE Anticipate the worst long before the dreaded event, but shortly before and during the event think positively and direct your thoughts to the specific task at hand.

Think Positive

Next, anticipate the event by picturing yourself in the actual situation. Visualize the scene, the persons, the physical surroundings, and the way you will be dressed. Tell yourself, "I am prepared to face any type of question, any reaction, because I have anticipated it." Imagine yourself calm and self-possessed, answering questions with ease or carrying your point with full control. See yourself dominating the situation: You are not vulnerable to individual responses or external interference. Pause and visualize yourself behaving the way you would like to in the future. This will help you when the anticipated moment comes. Positive thinking improves performance and leads to success. Winners use it all the time.

Task-Oriented Thinking

In Chapter 5 you will learn specific methods to facilitate recall. Keeping your mind on the task will appear much easier once you know what to do. As you stop dwelling on your anxiety, you can start thinking. Ask questions; organize and analyze the task at hand. Keep your mind busy with the question "How could I perform the task?" This will prevent or dissipate anxiety. Keep to the task, not to the worries.

Anxiety Reduction with Music

Listening to slow pieces of baroque music has a soothing effect on the mind and can thus enhance the recording part of memory. The Lozanov method of learning is based on reading the information to be remembered in a certain tempo with a musical background of about 60 beats a minute (the same as a largo movement). You simply pace what you want to say into a certain length of time, which alternates with silence. The more relaxed you become, the better your concentration will be. For example, you want to learn a word in French. Listen to the music for four beats, and then say aloud during the next four beats: "railroad station: *la gare.*"

1 - 2 - 3 - 4   1 - 2 - 3 - 4
(Listen to the music.)   "Railroad station: *la gare.*"

The Lozanov method aims at integrating unconscious and conscious processes in a harmonious way, supposedly to facilitate memorization. It is still controversial although it has given satisfactory results in elementary schools in Bulgaria. It is applied mainly to foreign language learning. It may indeed prove useful to learn vocabulary by rote, but analytic methods give more in-depth knowledge. One is better off combining several techniques than using just one.

Listen to the slow movement of any baroque piece and repeat a sentence you want to remember. Feel relaxed, in control, and in harmony with the music. (You can choose a verse, a famous line, a fortune cookie message, an ad, something a friend said, a proverb, etc.) Here are a few sentences I find interesting enough to memorize:

- "Men live by forgetting; women live on memories."
  —*T. S. Eliot*

- "We forget because we must and not because we will."—*Matthew Arnold*

- "Memory like women is usually unfaithful."—*Spanish proverb*

- "Women are as old as they feel; men are old when they lose their feelings."—*Mae West*
- "Life is all memory, except for the one present moment that goes by so quick you hardly catch it going." —*Tennessee Williams*
- "The word 'impossible' is not in my dictionary." —*Napoleon*
- "Most of the disorders and evils in life are the result of man's inability to sit still and think."—*Pascal*

Quick Review

1. Relaxation reduces anxiety, which is one of the major causes of memory disturbances.
2. Relaxation improves attention. It allows you to pause, be aware, and concentrate.
3. Progressive muscle relaxation with visualization relaxes the body and the mind.
4. Rhythmic breathing relieves excess tension and allows better concentration.
5. Anxiety-reduction exercises help control anxiety and improve concentration.
6. Relaxation helps you deal with anxiety on the physical level, clearing the way to memory.
7. Knowledge about memory function, awareness, and a positive attitude help you deal with anxiety on a psychological level, freeing the way to concentration.
8. Task-oriented thinking relieves anxiety by replacing negative thoughts. Instead of dwelling on how poorly you expect to do, you think about a way to perform the task.

PART 2

Improving Concentration

CHAPTER 5

Imagery and Visualization

"A thing of beauty is a joy forever."

Keats

Imagery

Long after irises have bloomed, long after loved ones have gone, we can play those special moments on the screen of the mind. Each time we call on imagery to visualize a scene from the past, we erase the sense of time from our consciousness and enjoy the eternal present of living memories. Whether it is to stimulate recall or to ensure long-term recording, one of the most precious ingredients in memory is the ability to think in terms of images, that is, to visualize what is perceived. Images have a concrete quality which gets the message across immediately and clearly. In order to remember abstract concepts, we must "bring them home," that is, work them into a context, or a frame of reference. Only then do we relate them to our lives and understand their relevance.

This is true even for mathematics, physics, and other sciences, which all involve the use of diagrams, graphics, formulas, and specific experiments. In philosophy, theories and principles are illustrated with references to everyday life. Descartes's metaphor of the wax tablet is an example: Hard and liquid, it looks like two different substances, yet it is one and the same. *Theory:* Beware of your senses; they may lead you astray. Only reason is the vehicle of truth. The philosophers we remember best are those who have turned their ideas into flesh.

Voltaire rebuked Leibniz's idealism with his wonderful and very readable tale *Candide, or Optimism*. Likewise, in literature reality takes on a new dimension, integrating the images of myths into everyday life. Superman is the image of people's yearning for superpower. He saves lives, helps the weak, and brings happiness through his magical stunts. These are concrete illustrations of the principle of power in the service of good. For him time and space are no obstacles: He can fly and be there as fast as he thinks. Our yearning to transcend the human condition has taken shape in Superman. Our language is full of idiomatic expressions stressing the necessity we feel to translate abstract thought into concrete images:

- Get the picture?
- Do you see what I mean?
- To frame or reframe a problem.
- To bring a problem down to manageable size.
- "A picture is worth a thousand words."

Images expressed in language, which are called metaphors, explain ideas in a direct way. They are very colorful in everyday speech as well as in literature. Some people have their own set of metaphors which reflect an individual world view, and there are also cultural metaphors which people often use unconsciously. In the United States, where baseball is the most popular sport, people often use expressions such as "get to first base." All images have the effect of getting the message across easily. They also add originality and even beauty to the expression of ideas. One day I was talking to an intelligent Japanese man about how imagery helps memory but how weird this sounds to the western mind. He told me that when he remembers something, it starts with mood, then images, never with ideas or logical constructs. We discussed the differences between western and eastern patterns of thought as reflected in language structure. In Japanese, for instance, there is no alphabet like ours but a series of signs people have to visualize first and conceptualize later. Also, the philosophy of life in Japan is more relaxed, more susceptible to mood, signs, and ritual. What is said is less important than the way one says it. Form has an importance which goes beyond the functional. It is also an aesthetic point of view which blends with the idea of harmony. Perhaps because Japan is a crowded group of islands, people learn very young to isolate themselves in their minds, using visualization and imagination. It is bound to help the memory, too.

If you have a vivid imagination, you will do well in this chapter. You will find out that you already own a mine of resources to help your memory. If you think you have none, you will discover that everyone, even you, can do it.

Here is an illustration of how to use imagery and integrate it in your life. Imagine and visualize the following:

1. A cat licking its paw
2. Tension in the city
3. Sadness at home

The first phrase is easy to visualize because it is a concrete image of an animal gesture everyone has actually seen. The second is more difficult because it is abstract: Tension does not provide one with a direct, concrete image. You have to look for one, using your imagination in order to translate tension into, say, the tense faces of harried New Yorkers hurrying through the streets of the city. What about the third phrase? Is it abstract or concrete? Does it bring a direct image or do you have to search for one? I think most people would agree that the third phrase is easier despite being abstract, because it relates to the familiar "home" each of us can visualize immediately. Thus, "sadness at home" is instantly translated into the image of a loved one feeling sad at home.

In his book about memory, Laird Cermak asks a few questions to help people find out whether they use imagery unconsciously. Try to answer them.

- Can you describe the layout of your house without visualizing it?

- Can you tell what objects are on your desk without closing your eyes and trying to picture the top of your desk?
- Name your five favorite ties or blouses. Did an image pop into your head as you named each object?

By becoming aware of your potential for imagery, you can improve the recording of your memories and their recall. Direct imagery comes to you directly. For example, when you think "sun," the image of the sun comes along instantly. It is built in. Indirect imagery, however, requires transformation from the abstract into a concrete form. Communism can be visualized in the symbol of the hammer and sickle. Love becomes a heart, peace a dove, and so forth.

Several mnemonic codes are based on imagery. You will read about them in Part III of this book. For example, the principle behind remembering numbers easily consists of translating the abstract signs into images and forming a cluster of them. It has been argued for centuries whether people have the innate ability to think and visualize at the same time: What came first, the idea of the chair or the image of the chair? No one knows for sure, but it is hard to create from sheer abstraction. An engineer always has an image—though sometimes rough and lacking detail—of what he or she wants to build. Often it is the function which creates the form: A chair has to support the weight of the body and give comfort, since we use it to rest. Creative thinking depends on visual imagination. It is the only way to bypass logical patterns which limit our reasoning. Einstein attributed his breakthrough formulation of the theory of relativity to the idle shuffling of images in his mind. Likewise, imagination creates rich memories. Remembering is a creative endeavor. You filter reality, select some elements, color them with your personality, and store them in a certain mood.

Using your imagination is a must for developing your ability to visualize. Psychologists have studied the mental processes of people with extraordinary memories and have found that most of them are gifted with a photographic memory which takes pictures of every stimulus perceived by the brain. Everybody has it to a certain degree in childhood. Young children learn first through their senses. Then, as they grow up and enter adulthood, they somehow switch modes and become more intellectually oriented. Those who have an extraordinary memory maintain this sensory ability throughout their lives. We can train children so that they do not lose it, and we can train ourselves to regain it. Imagination plays a big role in the formation of images. Use yours freely.

Visualization

Everyone knows instinctively how to visualize, but let's analyze the process to make the most of it. To visualize is to recreate in your mind a picture of an object you have seen or imagined in the past. Here we are concerned with a picture that is observed with care and without rushing, since our purpose is memorization.

When we visualize something, we project on the screen of our minds the image of an object as we perceived it. While doing this, we review in detail the elements which struck our attention as we were looking and concentrating. In order to get a clear mental picture of something, you must close your eyes and, while relaxing, try to focus on the image you have assimilated. It will be the result of your personal observation and will include detailed information on shape, size, color, texture, mood, and so forth. At this moment your mind is active, not passive, and you are recording the memory you have chosen to store.

Visualization has been used for centuries by philosophers and mystics eager to attain peace of mind. They simply recreated in their minds an ideal picture which they associated with serenity. As they focused all their attention on this image, they noticed that they felt relaxed and in tune with their senses. Prisoners have used it to keep up their morale and their sanity in solitary confinement. Nowadays, the same technique is used in psychotherapy to induce relaxation and help create a positive image. Since the main idea is to focus attention on a clear image and carry it in the mind long after it has been perceived by the senses, this is a good technique for memory training.

You can train yourself to visualize what you read, taste, smell, and even hear. For instance, when you make a phone call, visualize the friend you are talking to. Ask some questions about where your friend is in the house and what he or she is doing, and imagine his or her body language, facial expressions, etc. If you want to remember when you must pick up your clothes at the cleaner's, focus on the ticket. The day of the week should be circled. Visualize it as you make a mental note of it. Your mind is a camera. Use it to translate experience into imagery.

Quick Review

You can improve your memory by learning how to use imagery. Thinking in terms of images can be enjoyable and rewarding.

A. Imagery

1. Concrete thinking helps memory.
2. Transform abstract ideas into concrete form, and you have an image.
3. Images conveying emotions are better remembered.
4. The more specific the image, the better.
5. Personalizing the context increases the emotional impact of the image.

B. Visualization

1. Visualization and imagery are essential to good memory.
2. Everyone has the ability to develop imagination skills.
3. Images which contain emotions and personal references stick better.

4. To visualize is to recreate a picture in your mind; it involves observation and image projection. It takes at least 15 seconds per item to be remembered, but it guarantees excellent recall.

Imagery Exercises

Here are a few tips. First, disregard the fear of ridicule. It will often interfere with the making of images. Second, test your distrust of the technique of image projection by trying it right away. Third, do not think this is a waste of time. It pays off like any organized behavior, e.g., looking at a map.

Exercise 1: Direct and Indirect Imagery

Visualize the following items and find out which are direct imagery and which are indirect imagery. Direct imagery is easy to visualize, whereas indirect imagery requires an effort of imagination.

1. A baby sleeping
2. A squirrel eating a nut
3. War in the middle east
4. A flooded area
5. Time passing slowly
6. A flaw in a fabric
7. A flaw in an argument
8. God
9. Mystery
10. King Kong
11. Hate
12. Love
13. Charity
14. Humor
15. Snow
16. Wood

Exercise 2: Imagery and Emotions

Close your eyes for better concentration and visualize the following:

1. A lion attacking a doe
2. A dog wagging her tail
3. A fly in your soup

4. A box of Valentine's Day chocolate in a red heart-shaped box
5. A flashlight in the dark (static, then moving)
6. A stain on your favorite shirt or blouse
7. A diamond gleaming in the sun
8. A scream of terror in the night
9. The joy of motherhood
10. A friend stealing money from your wallet

Do not reread. Get a piece of paper and try to "see" which images you remember. Write them down. When you are finished, analyze them and identify the emotions they convey. Then compare your list with the original and draw your own conclusions. Which images and which emotions stuck in your memory? You may want to test your memory again later, tomorrow, or at the end of the week. You will be surprised.

Exercise 3:   Imagery and Intensity of Emotion

Close your eyes and visualize the following images:

1. a beehive
    a beehive at your door
    a wasp's nest in your bathroom
2. a very sharp knife
    a very sharp knife cutting a thick steak
    a very sharp knife cutting your finger
3. an old man sitting on a bench
    an old man sitting on a bench in the sun
    an old man sitting on a bench in the sun, weeping
4. a rainbow against a stormy sky
    a rainbow above your house against a stormy sky
    a rainbow above your house against a stormy sky, cheering
       you up
5. a bird pecking in the garden
    a bird bathing in a pool of water
    a bird escaping the attack of a cat

6. leaves falling from a tree
   red and yellow leaves falling from a tree
   red and yellow leaves falling from a tree on your lawn

7. a broken jar on your kitchen floor
   a broken jar of cranberries on your kitchen floor
   a broken jar of cranberries on your kitchen floor at night

8. an ambulance flashing and wailing in the street
   an ambulance flashing and wailing by your house
   an ambulance flashing and wailing at your doorstep

Do not reread. Take a piece of paper and write down all the images you remember. Check your answers and ask yourself which kinds of images you tend to remember better.

Exercise 4:   Your Favorite Recipes

You can use visualization to help remember cooking recipes, provided that you are familiar with the process. If you have never been active in the kitchen, you do not have any file in your mind to store recipes. You do not have any frame of reference, and it will be much harder to remember. However, try it, for imagery is a powerful engraver of memories.

1. Visualize the ingredients separately (later on, with practice, you will be able to visualize them in the given proportions).

2. Visualize the different steps. Imagine yourself mixing ingredients, chopping, etc., while visualizing the process.

Use a simple recipe to start with. Read it first and then visualize it step by step, in ''scenes.'' In the following chapters you will learn how to combine visualization with other organizational techniques, and this exercise will be perfected. For the time being, just try to remember images of ingredients and steps.

Example: Learning how to bake beer bread

Measure

   3 cups of self-rising flour
   3 tablespoons of sugar
   1 12-ounce can of beer

Mix the ingredients lightly. Pour at once into a well-greased bread pan. Bake in a 375-degree oven for 45 minutes.

NOTE Use your imagination and choose familiar references to make your images. For instance, visualize first the 3 cups of flour "self-rising" over the brim of the cup. You'll remember the image which includes proportions and special ingredients. Then visualize a 12-ounce can of beer of the brand you usually buy. You'll remember better a specific brand you enjoy. Notice the following rule:

Clear images of objects you personally relate to are better remembered.

Thus, always visualize a particular object (e.g., Michelob beer).

It will become as concrete as possible and will register better.

Visualization Exercises

In the following exercises, we proceed from simple figures to more complex ones and finally to people's faces.

Exercise 1: Mental Images of Beauty and Harmony

Think of your mind as a screen onto which you can project all your fantasies. Use your imagination to enrich your everyday life. You can change your mood through visualization. You can relax or feel tense according to which image you choose to focus on.

1. Sit in a comfortable chair in a peaceful place.
2. Close your eyes and visualize an image which evokes peace and quiet to you, for example, the sun setting over the hills or the sea. Form a clear picture in your mind.
3. Observe the beauty of the scenery (the color of the sky and the hills or sea).
4. Notice how your breathing is shallow, how you feel in harmony with yourself and your environment. Be aware of your moods and feelings.

Do this exercise with several mental images. You will be able to recreate scenery you like and beautiful objects you have seen, thus bringing back happy experiences to your consciousness. Try a mountain lake, a cat dozing, green pastures, or a flower close up.

Exercise 2:   Pictures

This exercise is based on observation of pictures or objects. Find your own in magazines, art books, antique shops, department stores, etc. Start with simple images and then move on to more complex ones.

1. Make sure you are feeling relaxed.
2. Look carefully at the picture for 2 minutes. It should be placed at a comfortable distance so that your eyes are not strained. Look at the shape and color of the picture. If your mind wanders, do not get nervous and upset. Just bring it back to the picture. This type of visual concentration takes time and practice. Keep your eyes on the picture.
3. Close your eyes and try to recapture the picture. You should see in your mind's eye exactly the same picture, but not as sharp as reality—something like a good copy of a bright sunset lingering in your mind.
4. Open your eyes and check to see if you have recaptured the entire picture. It should be a clear mental image.

NOTE Do not expect to see an image as sharp as reality or you will be disappointed. The point is to see it as clearly as possible. If your first attempt was not successful, do not despair. Give yourself more time and try again. As you improve, decrease the observation time from 2 minutes to 1 minute. Remember that patience and practice are the keys to success.

Exercise 3: Observation and Mental Rotation

Start observing real objects from different perspectives, walking around them and looking at them from above and underneath. Next, close your eyes and visualize every different angle. You will then find it easier to imagine without actually observing.

1. Imagine an object seen from different angles: from above, from behind, from the left, from the right.

2. Imagine a picture seen from different perspectives as if you were a photographer considering different angles.

3. Do the same with a sculpture or any object you have seen recently.

4. Choose a familiar place (garden, tree, street) and imagine it in different seasons.

5. Choose a few rooms in your house and imagine them at different times of day. Visualize the different light, temperature, and mood.

6. Think of a person you know very well. Visualize that person seen from the back, the front, and in profile. Imagine the person sitting: reading, watching television, eating at the table. Then imagine the person in motion: walking, going up or down the stairs, getting in and out of a car, smiling, sad, etc. Think about gestures, demeanor, and attitudes.

Exercise 4: Faces

Visualize a face. Then move to a real face when you meet someone or see a person on television. Do you manage to recreate the picture in your mind? Check yourself by describing the characteristics of that face.

NOTE This type of exercise is easier for some people than for others. Some people are predominantly visual, while others are predominantly verbal. Observing and visualizing will become second nature, and you will have an easier time remembering.

Exercise 5:   A Live Scene

Visualize an incident that you witnessed at home, in a store, or on the street, e.g., a woman having her purse snatched or a car accident or just a lovely person or a happy scene.

Exercise 6:   Poems

Try to visualize the following poem by Wordsworth. Visualize each line as you read it; then close your eyes and recapture the images in the poem. (Fifteen years after learning it at school, I still carry its beautiful imagery in my mind: those golden daffodils fluttering and dancing in the breeze.) Do the same with "The Tyger" by William Blake and "Autumn Sickly" by Apollinaire.

Daffodils

I wandered lonely as a cloud
That floats on high o'er vales and hills,
When all at once I saw a crowd,
A host, of golden daffodils;
Beside the lake, beneath the trees,
Fluttering and dancing in the breeze.

Continuous as the stars that shine
And twinkle on the milky way,
They stretched in never-ending line
Along the margin of a bay:
Ten thousand saw I at a glance,
Tossing their heads in sprightly dance.

The waves beside them danced; but they
Out-did the sparkling waves in glee:
A poet could not but be gay,
In such a jocund company:
I gazed—and gazed—but little thought
What wealth the show to me had brought:

For oft, when on my couch I lie
In vacant or in pensive mood,
They flash upon the inward eye
Which is the bliss of solitude;
And then my heart with pleasure fills,
And dances with the daffodils.

William Wordsworth (1804)

The Tyger

Tyger, tyger, burning bright,
In the forests of the night:
What immortal hand or eye,
Could frame thy fearful symmetry?

In what distant deeps or skys
Burnt the fire of thine eyes?
On what wings dare he aspire?
What the hand, dare seize the fire?

And what shoulder, & what art,
Could twist the sinews of thy heart?
And when thy heart began to beat,
What dread hand? & what dread feet?

What the hammer? what the chain,
In what furnace was thy brain?
What the anvil? what dread grasp,
Dare its deadly terrors clasp?

When the stars threw down their spears
And water'd heaven with their tears:
Did he smile his work to see?
Did he who made the Lamb make thee?

Tyger, tyger, burning bright,
In the forests of the night:
What immortal hand or eye,
Could frame thy fearful symmetry?

William Blake (1794)

Autumn Sickly

O ill beloved Autumn
Thou shalt die when the hurricane
    breathes in rose gardens
When the snow has fallen
in the orchards

O sorry Autumn
die then in whiteness and fecundity
of snow and ripened fruit
In the well of the sky
the sparrow hawks soar
over the green haired nixes and dwarfs
who have never loved

On the edge of distant woods
stags have trumpeted

Season I love thy ghostly cries I love
your fruit that falls to no collecting hand
the forest and the wind that shed
leaf by slow leaf your tears upon the ground
The leaves
beaten down

the trains
that run
as life
flows on

Guillaume Apollinaire
(Translated by John C. Lapp)

CHAPTER 6

Sensory Awareness

"since feeling is first . . ."

e.e. cummings

The notions of attention, concentration, and awareness all refer to our perceptions of reality. We perceive the world through our senses before our minds start to process the information and store it in our memory banks. Through our senses we intercept thousands of stimuli which trigger in us several kinds of reactions, both emotional and intellectual. When we become aware of them, we are helping our memory. While making a note of what we perceive, we are controlling the recording process.

Unfortunately, we do not usually pay much attention to our senses. Perhaps it is cultural. In western civilization, philosophers, scientists, and religious authorities have conspired to present the senses as an unreliable, hence dangerous, source of information. We are taught to disregard them as soon as we are past infancy. We are taught to think beyond them and in spite of them. The result is inner conflict, an uneasy feeling about nature itself from a moral point of view. We step out of this trap by giving it as little thought as possible. The consequences for memory should not be understated. By ignoring them, we shrink our potential for memory.

Rediscovering the Senses

My aim is to make you rediscover your senses the way you experienced them as a child but with the awareness of an adult. Once you learned how to relate to the world through feeling, touch, sound, and image. It was a powerful way of remembering a lot of information in a short period of time. You learned your mother language by mimicking sounds and relating them to images. Babies learn about conflict through the quarrels and screams of their siblings or parents. Abstraction does not exist yet for them, only pure sensation. As we mature, we tend to consider sensations as abstract—because they are difficult to define, I guess. Abstract or not, our senses work wonders for memory. The focus is on the emotional. It is not clear how it works, but even stroke victims suffering from aphasia can remember words through perception. One such woman could not say the word "snow," but it came back to her when she touched the real thing. What these people cannot retrieve otherwise is often given to them free by their senses. Unfortunately, they tend to forget again and again and have no control over memory.

Freud observed that "we remember what interests us." We spend the necessary time and effort to look, listen, and feel only if we are interested in something or someone. No matter what the reason is for this lack of attention, we can correct it if we have true motivation to do so. You are already motivated enough since you are reading this book. This chapter will include exercises on sensory awareness which will make you realize that the senses are the best allies in helping you remember. Trust them, and your memory will improve.

The more sensory perceptions that are involved, the more likely it is that you will remember something or someone. For instance, if you really look at a flower, you do more than see it. You become active, receptive to its size, shape, color, texture, and scent. The more information you have, the better you will remember it. Notice that in order to properly observe, you must spend time. Many people think that they should remember something instantly, as if by magic. When they are absorbed in doing a task they enjoy, they are unaware of the passage of time and of their degree of concentration. They seem to believe that it is an unconscious process quite foreign to conscious effort. In truth, though it is an unconscious process for many people, it follows a pattern which can be consciously learned and reinforced. Increasing your sensory awareness will add to the quality of your life. Thus be open, receptive, and curious and choose material that you enjoy to practice what you learn in this course. As Professor Leon Michaux has observed, we remember

1. What is useful (we use it all the time)
2. What we perceive in context (it makes sense we relate to)
3. What is pleasant (we are involved emotionally and concentrate easily)
4. Actions that have been interrupted (we review and organize)

Using Your Senses

Auditory memory, one of the oldest memory techniques, makes use of the rhythm and rhyme of speech. Ancient people developed this technique to remember stories, legends, and religious lore. You can use it to enhance your verbal memories. About 40 percent of the population is predominantly "verbal." These individuals are sensitive to words, rhymes, and sounds. Spontaneously they think of puns and verbal associations. Everyone can improve verbal skills. You need not reach the inspired heights of Homer; any use of rhyme and rhythm will help you remember. Even rhymes that are artistically crude can have a powerful effect on memory. Examples of this are the simple advertising jingles that run through your head. They are not great poetry, but, combined with simple tunes, they do stick, don't they? Think of a few, and you will be surprised at how they pop out of your mind: Can you sing "Gentlemen prefer Hanes''? For an exercise to help you learn verbal memory techniques, make a shopping list of six items and make simple rhymes or limericks out of three of them. Tuck the list in your pocket and see if you don't remember better the ones for which you found rhymes.

Kinesthetic memory, or "muscle memory," is the kind of memory we all use to perform actions from such commonplace activities as walking to dancing or playing concert piano. This type of memory is most sensitive to practice and repetition and is usually preverbal. You can use it to rehearse things you want to say or do in a certain way. Find a place with some room to move around, think of a motion or movement that is connected with whatever you want to remember, and perform that movement. For example, if you want to remember a song or a few lines of a play or movie, do what actors do: Go through the physical motions and feel the emotions through your body. Try to imitate gestures and voice. Rehearsing involves much more than repetition. In involves feelings as well as thoughts. Thus, you will be able to remember important words, such as Clark Gable's last line in *Gone with the Wind:* "Frankly, my dear, I don't give a damn!" Say it aloud, thinking about Scarlett, imagining her tense face as you stand at the door and turn away from her. If you actually do it and use vocalization, you will remember better since acoustic traces remain longer in memory. It may help to exaggerate the motion. For example, if you are trying to remember a key, use your body and muscles to develop a kinetic image by turning a large imaginary key in a lock. Play with using body language: Turn off the stove with emphasis, bending to look at each knob and pointing at it in the off position. Do it consciously with the purpose of remembering better. It can be like mime or dancing. You may even find it enjoyable.

Visual memory, also called photographic memory, may be the most useful of all; indeed, most memory systems are based on it. Most people (60 percent) are predominantly visual, although few have developed this skill to the utmost. Artists, photographers, craftspersons, and others in the visual arts use it in their work, but only "mnemonists"—that is, people with extraordinary memories—use it in all the contexts of their lives to remember all kinds of information. They have devised their own memory systems based on image association. Years of research have proved that anyone can improve visual skills at any age, because we all have the potential ability to visualize. In the chapters on imagery and absentmindedness, you will find many applications. Here is an example that combines visual and kinesthetic memory. Say you want to remember that you locked all the windows and doors before you left your house. Proceed systematically from room to room and close the windows and doors with precise gestures. Take a mental picture of each gesture you perform consciously. You will "see" yourself in the different places, and you will "feel" the different efforts each one requires (e.g., you'll note, "Window in blue room now closed; always difficult to reach across the desk"). Sensory awareness will guarantee that you remember all the gestures you do consciously.

I've illustrated these examples using only three sensory modalities, but the senses of smell and taste can also increase the chances of recall considerably. The more senses involved in recording a memory, the better. It is like fishing with cues to catch memories. When you cast a line with five hooks, you have a better chance to catch a fish, haven't you? It is the same with memory. Learn to plant cues with your senses; the results will surprise you.

Quick Review

1. Sensory awareness is the first step to brain activity and hence to memory. If nothing is recorded, nothing can be recalled. Make sure you do not blame your memory for your lack of attention.

2. Pause and perceive actively: look, listen, touch, taste, smell, move. Develop your sensory awareness, and you will easily compensate for the decline in perception which may occur with age.

3. Combining all sensory modes will give the best results.

Exercises

Exercise 1:   Awareness

To do this exercise, you will need a writing pad, a pencil, and a timer. Figure 6-1 contains 12 images. Concentrate on the top row for 30 seconds, covering the rest with a piece of paper to make it easier to focus on only those three images. When the

Figure 6-1

minute has passed, cover the whole page and try to draw the images as well as you can from memory. Look back at the originals and check to see if they are exactly the same. Then move on to the next row. Finally, challenge yourself by trying the last two rows together.

Exercise 2: Awareness of Visual Detail

You will find four graphics in Figure 6-2. Look at each for 1 minute, hiding the others for better concentration. Visualize it well. Then try to reproduce the graphic on a piece of paper.

Exercise 3: Awareness of Verbal Material

The purpose of this exercise is to heighten your awareness of each of the items in the following lists (study one at a time). When a word has several meanings, choose one or use all the meanings for more practice. As you read each word, imagine how the object looks, smells, sounds, tastes, and feels. Use your imagination, and you will remember the lists. For example, toothpaste looks glossy and green, smells of synthetic mint, and tastes of sweet synthetic mint. Skip any sense which does not apply (in this case, sound).

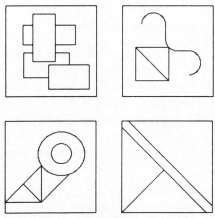

Figure 6-2

Paper	Cane	Handkerchief
Vanilla	Kiss	Boot
Movie	Knot	Tear
Trolley	Cart	Finger
Racket	Cat	Crepe
Hair	Surf	Nutmeg
Shoe	Licorice	Country
Wheel	Doctor	Orchid
Happiness	Elephant	Bird
Silk	Cotton	Wool

Exercise 4:   Awareness of Visual Material

Find pairs of pictures, such as comic strips. Practice finding the differences between the two. You can do the same thing by looking at two similar items: two cars, two garments, etc.

Exercise 5:   Awareness and Smell

Carefully smell flowers, branches, perfumes, cooking—anything you can put your nose on. Analyze the specific odor and try to describe it. Compare it with another. Think about your preferences, what you enjoy and what puts you off. Ask yourself why this is so. After a while you will find it very easy to put these feelings into words.

Exercise 6:   Awareness and Taste

Carefully taste the food on your plate at mealtime. (Do not smoke at the table, because smoking dulls the sense of taste.) Analyze the particular flavor of each item. Become aware of how seasonings and spices modify the taste of food. Guess about the ingredients in the recipe. Compare it with another food of the same category (i.e., two jams, chocolates, cuts of meat, fish). As you practice, you will enjoy food a lot more.

NOTE   In order to activate your tastebuds, you must roll and press your tongue against the vault of your palate. You will taste food and drink better if you savor them for a few seconds before swallowing. (A good training for your sense of taste and smell is wine tasting.)

Exercise 7: Awareness and Hearing

Music Listen carefully to a favorite song or piece of music. Try to catch the words or the tune. Analyze it, follow the melody, try to identify the instruments, follow the part each plays, listen for recurring refrains, listen to the moods expressed, and identify the different tempos in each movement.

Tunes, Noises, and Sounds Listen carefully to a bird's song. Analyze it: What is the pitch (high or low notes)? Is it grating or smooth, simple or complex? Follow the melody, the tempo, the pauses. Try to imitate it. Break it down into units, using musical notation or a diagram. Compare it with the song of another bird. Analyze and identify other noises you hear.

Words and Expressions Listen to the sound of words. Many imitate their meaning (e.g., buzz, hiss, tweet). This is called onomatopoeia, and it is widely used in poetry. Try to rhyme words with the items you want to remember (e.g., lox stocked in a box).

Dialogue Listen better to what people say and how they say it. Analyze message, language, manner, and mood. Do they express themselves in a direct way or beat around the bush? What is their choice of words? What is their tone of voice?

Exercise 8: Awareness of Daily Actions

Become aware of what you do and how you do it. Remember once and for all details which irritate you and make you blame your memory. I used to fiddle with my sandal straps the way an ape would, each time trying randomly to find the right hole: many frantic gestures and little thought. One day I decided to remember which holes were most comfortable. I counted them and visualized them on the left ankle and the right ankle. Starting from the end of the strap, I counted fourth hole on the left, third on the right. It worked! Now I remember because I made a conscious, organized recording. I go directly for the right holes.

Do the same thing to remember light switches in your home. Find your own exercises by thinking about your frustrations. Pause, analyze the situation, make a mental note of it, and visualize it; you will stop blaming your memory.

Exercise 9:   Visual Awareness

You will be more efficient as you become more visually aware. Observe traffic lights at a main intersection and try to figure out the pattern. You will be able to anticipate how long the red lights last. As a result you may discover the quickest routes. Notice street signs in your neighborhood and make it a point to remember a few intersections. Unless you do, they will not register and you will have only a vague idea of the location. This can save you the embarrassment of not knowing the name of the street next to yours.

Exercise 10:   Awareness of Color

Expand your sensory awareness by looking at colors and analyzing them. There are so many nuances in every color: Consider the different shades of each primary color (*e.g.,* poppy red, cherry red), degrees of clarity (bright, toned down, subdued), and value (dark or light). When you go shopping, look at fabrics or garments and compare their colors. Look for harmonies of tone and value as well as shade. You will notice that color, mood, and personality are related. When you are outdoors look at the different colors in nature: sky, clouds, earth, grass, leaves, tree bark, flowers. Enjoy the variety!

NOTE   You can teach yourself color awareness by mixing primary colors (red, yellow, blue). Look at a color chart and start experimenting.

CHAPTER 7

Selective Attention

*"An object **once attended to** will remain in memory, whereas one inattentively allowed to pass will leave no traces."*

William James

Selective attention refers to the ability to be *attentive* to whatever you *select* to concentrate on. This selective process is essential for good memory performance. At school and at work, the selection of what is important is often made for us. We are told to study something specific, and we do it easily, without noticing that this selection allows us to concentrate automatically on what's essential. When we are on our own, we must make the decision. Unconsciously we sift what we need to survive and leave the rest to chance. You gain control of your memory by carefully choosing the things you consider to be worth remembering.

As you observe the object of your attention, there is a second selection at work. What have you singled out? Are you aware of analyzing something in particular? It is only after you have asked yourself the question "What is it I find worth remembering?" that you will develop the habit of focusing consciously on what is important to you. For instance, if you want to remember individuals in a peer group, do not dwell on resemblances like the depressed lady who complained, "I cannot remember people in the nursing home. They all look alike: gray-haired and wrinkled." The fact is that no two heads of hair are alike (different shades, textures, and hairdos), and there is an astonishing variety of wrinkle patterns. Be efficient and select differences rather than common characteristics to focus on. Then make it a point to remember them. Studies have shown that people do not automatically remember things. The desire for learning must be consciously expressed. For instance, a person did not remember a series of numbers shown to him no matter how many times he read it. Puzzled, the man's psychologist suddenly realized that she had neglected to ask him to learn these numbers. Once he was told to do so, he did remember. The mind needs specific directions in order to focus on remembering. Conscious recording helps recall.

What if you cannot decide what to select? Then you must arbitrarily choose to concentrate on something that interests you. Focus on one thing at a time, narrowing your selection to what you find most striking. If you have trouble defining it, just pick anything you notice and you will start processing it. It is important to act and thus shorten all the hesitations which prevent you from concentrating.

As we grow older, this becomes more difficult to achieve because we lose some of the ability to select the sensation we consider most important. We tend to give equal attention to everything and are more easily distracted. When this is combined with an inability to relax under stress and a reduced ability to form detailed, accurate sensory impressions, attention and concentration may become impaired. Attention deficits account for about 50 percent of reported memory problems. You can do exercises to improve selective attention and concentration and thus develop observation skills. "Skill in concentration is acquired, not inherited," Francis Robinson reminds us.

Emotional Awareness

In Chapter 6, "Sensory Awareness," you learned how important it is to focus on the senses as a first step in grasping information about something in which you are interested. Instead of looking at an object—a picture, for example—in a diffuse way, unaware of what is going on in your mind, you should pay attention to how you perceive it. Asking yourself, "How would it feel? How would it smell? How would it taste? How would it sound?" encourages you to do precisely that. Once you are considering an object from this basic angle, you are not passively seeing it. Instead, you are actively controlling what is worth noticing, deciding whether you want to record it in long-term memory.

Following the pattern in which our minds process information, we shall select to concentrate on what seems most *striking* in the object. This is an impressionistic approach, which means that it is your own impressions that count. Simply respond spontaneously to your instinct, name the particular feature, and then analyze it further. At this point you have selected to be attentive to your senses and to the feature that impresses you. This subjective process helps you store it more efficiently in your memory, for we seem to remember better what we feel deeply and what we consciously record as impressive.

The next step is to focus your attention on your emotions. When considering an object, try to become aware of its mood and how it affects you. Ask yourself, "Do I find it pleasant or unpleasant? Irritating or soothing? Shocking or plain? Sad or joyful? Scary or reassuring? Stimulating or boring?" Project this emotion back onto the object and ponder it for a few seconds. This ensures a better recording.

Professor Gordon Bower of Stanford University has done extensive research on mood and memory. "Your mood has a direct effect on which information you bring to mind to make a judgment. . . . Memory seems mood dependent: if the mood is negative, there is a higher availability of negative memories," he reports. This explains the cycle of depression in which one sad thought triggers another. This matching of moods can be induced consciously to control recall. Recapturing a vague emotion (anger, joy, excitement, sorrow) can lead you back to specific, more detailed memories.

Rational Awareness

Now we shall consider the object (or picture) from an intellectual angle, using reason instead of emotion. Simple organization can help a person focus on the essential and significant aspects of the picture.

1. Look at the whole picture and identify its subject or topic. In other words, select the essential message.

2. Notice the structure of the picture. Look at the colors, the background, the foreground, the exact location of the main subject. Here you record the subject in its spatial context.

3. Select the significant elements that give you specific information about the message. Here you are going one step further, zooming in on particular details. By commenting on a dress or a car in the picture, you record the subject in its temporal context and learn about the artist's individual "style," which can be defined as "difference from the norm." This step can be more or less elaborate according to how much detail you wish to record; for example, learning new material requires greater depth of processing.

If you combine all your resources using your senses, emotions, and your intellect, you will achieve maximum control over the recording process. Efficient recording is the key to good recall. It is up to you to decide what you want to remember. As soon as you have made this basic selection, follow the above outline and proceed from emotional toward rational awareness.

This may seem complicated at first because we are analyzing the different steps which are usually perceived as a single mental operation. In fact, it is quite simple. It will take very little time to follow the above outline, and it will guarantee satisfaction. You will be consciously doing what is efficient instead of leaving it to chance. As Francis Robinson reminds us, "A person is efficient not because of will power . . . but rather because he has developed habitual patterns or sequences of activities." With practice, thinking strategies will become second nature; you will be amazed at your improvement.

Observation Training with Pictures

Imagine that your mind is a camera focusing on different aspects of a scene. A great photographer uses sensory awareness to the utmost and then selects what he or she finds most interesting. Technical knowledge allows him or her to get a picture which reflects what he or she sees and feels. Ansel Adams said that a great picture is one that captures the mood perceived by the viewer at that particular moment. The same is true for memory: A great memory recaptures the original mood of a particular moment.

In the exercises you will teach yourself how to improve your observation skills through selecting to look at a series of pictures in an organized way. I have chosen paintings by Edouard Manet, which you will find on the following pages. I shall illustrate the method with the portrait of Émile Zola (Figure 7-1), and in the exercises you will try on your own with *Olympia* (Figure 7-2).

Analyzing the Whole Picture

Look at the whole picture. Get a general feel for it. Do you like it? Read the title and the name of the painter. Both can give you a general idea of the picture. If you know them, your associations will be added to your observations. Consider this a bonus, not a must. Look at the structure of the painting, that is, the layout: What is the central figure? What is in the foreground? Consider the essential first. Here we have a man sitting at a desk; we can assume it is his desk because of his easy, relaxed posture. His face has a thoughtful expression, and he is looking toward the right. Now consider the background. Above the desk, in the upper-right corner, several pictures appear in a

Figure 7-1

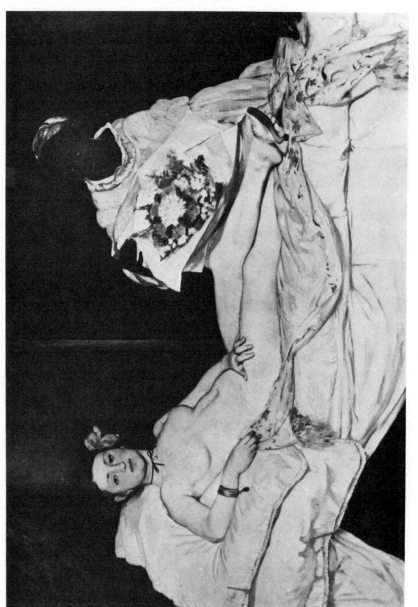

Figure 7-2

horizontal frame. One painting portrays a nude woman lying on a couch; next to it is another painting, vertical, of a Japanese warrior. On the left, behind the chair on which Zola is sitting, there is one panel of a Japanese divider screen with a motif of tree blossoms and bird. Now visualize the structure by closing your eyes. Do you appreciate the way the painter has framed the main character, placing him in his context? Look at the light. Where does it fall? Which elements are enhanced by it? Here it falls in the center of the picture: the white pages of the book Zola is holding. His face and hands are also included in this imaginary circle of light. If you have a color print of the painting available, look at the colors; describe them to yourself and comment on how you react to them. Dark brown tones fill the background of the picture: the furniture and the floor. White and beige stand out in the light, as does the yellow in the vertical panel.

Analyzing Details: Subjective Analysis

What strikes you in this portrait? Analyze what attracts you. Zoom in on it and then examine it in detail. There is no limit to your personal observation. You'll stop when you have taken in everything that interests you, but you will have recorded it with precision for further reference.

Analyzing Details: Objective Analysis

If you wish to learn about art or if you like this picture and want to record in your memory as much detail as possible simply because, as Keats wrote, "A thing of beauty is a joy for ever," proceed to analyze it even more thoroughly. Be systematic and select details. First examine the central figure, then the foreground, and finally the background. Here Zola is wearing a dark jacket with a white shirt. (Only the cuffs with gold cuff links show.) His pants are a greenish gray with a black stripe along the side, in the fashion of the day. (The same color is echoed in the desk, screen, and pictures.) Zola looks comfortable in his cozy study. He is seated on a padded chair covered with rich cloth. Brass studs add luster to its frame. His posture?

One leg is crossed, with one hand resting on it; the other hand is holding a book. Zola's gaze follows his profile position toward the right. He is pensive. On the desk are books, a pamphlet entitled *Manet,* and a quill pen in a porcelain inkwell. Pause and think: Be receptive to your reactions and comments. Dwell on them for better recording.

Did you notice several references to Manet? A sketch of his *Olympia* and his name on a book cover divert attention from Zola. This is not a traditional portrait with an empty background. Although dark background colors were chosen to enhance the face in the classic manner of the Dutch painters, this portrait is very active. It reveals the friendship between Manet and Zola, who defended each other against the critics. This work was controversial in its time, since it proved to be a personal and aesthetic statement.

Synthesis

What stands out? What mood does the painting express? Try to make a personal synthesis of your emotional and rational awareness. Bring together your impressions and your careful analysis. What is the mood in this picture? What struck you? What pleased you most? What would you like to remember?

Close your eyes and visualize the picture. Notice what stands out clearly in your mind's eye. This is what you have recorded carefully and consciously. You will remember a copy of the picture you just reconstructed. It may weaken in time. Therefore, make it crisp, moving, and memorable. Review it now and then.

How to Apply Awareness to Your Everyday Life

In the preceding section a specific picture was discussed as the most practical example for observation. It goes without saying that this basic method for observation can be applied to anything you would like to remember: a movie, a play, an episode of everyday life, a conversation, an accident, an incident in a store, and so forth. The principles taught here are generally applicable, and with practice you can develop your observation skills so that you will remember what you consider important anywhere and in any circumstances. As you exercise, you will be acquiring efficient conditioned reflexes, facilitating memory.

If called upon, you may be a useful eyewitness. Whenever you concentrate on rational analysis, you focus your attention on objective features such as size, color, shape, smell, sound, and context. These kinds of details are important for identifying lost objects or criminals. They can also help in assessing who was at fault in an accident. Incidentally, most eyewitness accounts conflict with one another and are not very reliable because people do not record *consciously* what they see. They do not analyze a situation systematically and in a detached manner. They rely on unconscious processes, which often distort one's perception of reality. If you have a curious mind, you raise questions and your mind is consciously active. You are then better equipped to make an objective assessment of a situation, taking into account your own biases. For example, our prejudices influence our judgments and our memories. Eyewitness tests in the United States have shown that people unconsciously distort what they actually see. In one experiment subjects were shown videotapes of dramatizations of crime. Half the crimes were committed by whites, and half were committed by nonwhites. However, the average subject reported that 80 percent of the criminals were nonwhites.

Get into the habit of paying more attention to what is going on around you. Making it a game is more fun. Imagine that you are a detective watching people's behavior or just become an observer of humankind and of nature. Shakespeare said, ''All the world's a stage,'' and it is. Try looking at it through the eyes of a director. For this you need only sharpen your observation skills. It may lead you to new hobbies and new discoveries. Photography, painting, drawing, and writing, like all creative activities, depend on awareness and close observation. The means of expression are technical tools which come later, as you get more interested in the subject and feel more self-confident. But the key to art, as Leonardo da Vinci said, is *sapere vedere*: to know how to look.

Train yourself by looking at objects; this is easy to do while shopping. In supermarkets, read labels. Become aware of the way they affect you: Do you like the packaging, its color, the picture on the box? Move from emotional awareness to rational awareness, analyzing the presentation of the product and reading the contents until you are satisfied. In department stores, look carefully at the items you intend to purchase. If you are trying on something, determine how you feel in it and then analyze the item, looking for flaws, checking that the pattern of the print is well matched at the seams, etc. Be systematic, starting at one end of the garment and working through each element in turn. You will become a better shopper, will have fewer frustrations, and will save time by not returning so many things. You may even save money by asking for price reductions on slightly flawed items.

DAILY GOAL Observe *one* object which draws your attention. Choose something you find pleasing, beautiful, or amusing. Be positive in your choice. For example, each time you visit friends, make it a point to notice something in their home and observe it carefully. Once back in your own home, try to visualize it and write it down (in your diary if you wish). The description of the object should be as detailed as possible. Mention it to your friends. They will be delighted you noticed.

The exercises in this chapter can be applied to almost anything. Get into the habit of comparing what you see. It will prove to be the springboard for many reflections on art, culture, personality, originality—all of what makes life interesting. We tend to look for common points when we want to unite or to conform. Stressing what all people have in common leads us to minimize the differences which divide them. However, when we are interested in the individual, we look for differences. Sometimes these become stereotyped into national, racial, or sexual characteristics. Juggling both similarities and differences and remaining constantly aware, we can prevent the excesses of prejudice. Because of all we have in common, we must learn

to live with our differences and appreciate them, too. Fortunately, we live in a free society in which differences are toler-
ated and often encouraged. Since highlighting differences helps
memory, you may be one step ahead.

Quick Review

To gain control over the recording of memories, we have to
become conscious of *what* we perceive, *how* we perceive it, and
how it *affects* us.
Selective attention allows you consciously to focus your
attention on what you select as important to record. It requires
emotional and rational awareness. Here are the elements in the
process of selective attention:

1. *Your senses:* How do you perceive the picture?
2. *Striking feature:* What strikes you in the picture?
3. *Your emotions:* How does this picture affect you?
4. *Your intellect:* Look for the following:

   - The *essential message:* the subject of the picture
   - The *structure* of the picture: its layout
   - The *significant elements:* details which illustrate the
     message

For everything you look at, ask yourself two basic questions: "Do I like it or not?" and "What is it I like or dislike?"
These questions will put you on the right track to process the
material deeply.

Analyzing a Picture: Selecting First the Whole, Then Details

You may want to review the section "Observation Training
with Pictures" before doing Exercise 1.

Exercise 1: *Olympia*

First, look at the whole picture and identify subject, place, and structure. Second, let yourself be guided by what strikes or interests you. Focus on it and analyze it in detail. Third, analyze the picture systematically, starting with the main characters or central subject and moving on to the foreground and the background. Scan the picture over and over, recording more details. Once you have the whole picture well in mind, make personal comments on it. Grasp all the associations that come to mind. Be sensitive to mood, color, texture, and your reactions. Pause on the characteristics of the artist's style, e.g., brushstrokes, colors (if possible), and favorite subjects. All these mental operations guarantee that you are processing this information for long-term retention. For best results, review it now and then.

You should be able to discover why *Olympia* was so controversial in the nineteenth century. Just look, feel, and think. After you have learned how to analyze a picture, you will have a much greater appreciation of what you see in shop windows, in stores, in waiting rooms, at your friends' homes, and in particular at an exhibition. The average viewer spends only 6 seconds looking at a painting according to a study measuring the attention span of people in a museum. Such a superficial glimpse does not leave an imprint on the mind. People remember only vaguely what they have seen without really looking. No wonder they remember so little: They do so little to remember! In contrast, art lovers, artists, and curious observers spend time recording what pleases and interests them; they analyze pictures in an organized way. You can do the same, increasing the quality of your life and your memory. Today *Olympia,* tomorrow the world!

Exercise 2: **Details and the Whole**

Study pictures of your choice in this manner. Go to the library and look for a book on your favorite subject. Think of a theme such as wild cats, butterflies, trees, fish, landscape painting, flower photography, portrait, or airplanes. Try to remember the pictures a few hours later and the next day. Describe them to yourself: first the whole picture, then details. Check yourself by going back to the picture. (If you write down your description, you will search for more details.)

Exercise 3: Looking versus Seeing

Divide a sheet of paper into two columns, one for pictures you will study and one for pictures you will just see superficially. Choose several pictures you like, five you will study, and five you will just see from a book, magazine, or exhibition. Start with pictures you think you know from having seen them many times, such as the *Mona Lisa, American Gothic, Whistler's Mother,* or a Marlboro cigarette ad. Give a title to each and write it in one of the columns. Describe it. A few hours later try to remember the pictures. Writing on a similar sheet of paper, compare the quality of your recall for the pictures you have studied and for the others. This will convince you that the method works.

Comparing: Analyzing Differences by Choosing a Theme

Comparing jogs the memory. In order to compare, you must have a good basic knowledge of at least one thing you will be comparing to another. Observing the relation between the two brings to mind personal associations. For example, say you are looking at books on cats because you are a cat lover. (Perhaps you are prospecting for the ideal cat.) Your own cat or a cat you have known is the standard reference you will use to compare others in terms of both physical characteristics and behavior. You may or may not have looked at your cat very closely. These exercises will encourage you to do so. You will become aware of typical markings or behavior patterns by studying those of other cats. Of course, you will analyze and categorize, which will result in good recollection of the subject—and perhaps even a better appreciation of your pet.

Exercise 1:   Differences within a Theme

First we are going to select a theme, or common subject, and see how different it can appear in pictures by artists with different personalities and cultural backgrounds. For example, everybody knows the characteristics of the female body. It has always been a favorite subject of painters, sculptors, photographers, and movie makers. Explore the ways in which it has been portrayed by a few great artists from different countries and in different periods.

Go to the library and look for one or several books on the subject. Study the pictures first, one at a time, looking for differences in expression, mood, shape of individual features, proportions, and background. Then look into the details of the face, hair, body, adornments, and so forth. Finally, take a general look at all the pictures and compare them. (Two by two is an easy way to proceed.) When you have finished your analysis, try to answer the following questions.

- What was the ideal of feminine beauty at different times in different places? Describe the characteristics of each and how they differ from one another. Be sensitive to expression and mood, since they reflect deep feelings and cultural characteristics.
- What is the difference between modern art and classical art?
- Which pictures do you like best? Why? How do they affect you?
- Have you learned something about woman, man, those different cultures, yourself?

For more practice, choose any theme you like and compare the different styles, e.g., paintings of Madonnas, children, landscapes, still lifes.

Exercise 2:   Flowers: Analyzing and Comparing by Looking for Differences

Choose some familiar as well as some exotic flowers. Taking walks in the spring is ideal for observing them on the stem. However, picture books with stunning photography are always available at the library. Ideally you should compare both and add paintings, fabrics, or anything with a flower motif. Here are some guidelines, using one of my favorite flowers: Would you be able to describe or draw an iris? You are no doubt familiar with this flower, yet you probably cannot say how many petals it has, what the structure of the flower is, where the colors mix, and where the blossoms grow on the stem. Of course, if you are an artist interested in flowers, you may have spent a lot of time observing, drawing, and painting them. Actually, few people work from memory nowadays, whereas before the nineteenth century all painters painted landscapes indoors, relying on memory.

First, if possible, study a real iris carefully. (You may discover, as I did by visiting an iris grower, that there are many different types of irises. Some are larger, others have long drooping petals, and others are bicolored. A few varieties have a wonderful scent.) It is important that you know the natural flower well in order to appreciate the differences in the art of painting flowers. There are a few lines, curves, and colors which are the trademark of a flower; these you will find in every artist's interpretation of a flower. They are its essence and the key to identification. Now analyze a picture of an iris. Work from emotional awareness to rational analysis. Ask yourself questions and try to answer them right away. Look at another picture of an iris. Compare it with the first one, noting the resemblances and differences. Concentrate on the differences. Do the same with other pictures of the same type of flower. Finally, try to remember the different flowers, visualizing them in as much detail as you can. Write down the characteristics of each one. You will be amazed to see how much you can teach yourself about art and nature just through careful observation.

Comparing: Analyzing Resemblances or Common Points

Art catalogs such as the one the Metropolitan Museum of Art sends before Christmas are ideal material with which to exercise your observation skills.

Exercise 1:   Catalog of a Current Exhibition

First, *analyze* pictures from the exhibition. *Compare* all the objects which you can group into categories, such as furniture, jewelry, sculpture, paintings, and fabrics. Look for *resemblances*. Comment on these art objects. Which decorative motifs or designs are common to the culture illustrated in this exhibition? Could they have a symbolic meaning like the cat in ancient Egypt? Observation may spur you to learn more about a subject.

Exercise 2:   Paintings of Your Choice

Individual Artists   Choose an exhibition or an art book of any famous painter. Look at several paintings by the same painter and analyze them carefully, looking for common elements. Is there a subject or theme dear to the painter's heart? How would you describe his or her paintings? Comment on color, texture, structure, expression, and mood.

Schools of Artists   Choose several painters with similar affinities and compare them. Look for resemblances but also for individual differences. For example, you might study impressionists, classic Dutch, Italian or Spanish masters, surrealists, cubists, expressionists, regionalists, primitives—there are many possibilities.

Comparing to Differentiate Similar Items

Look for any series of items on the same subject (for example, any artist's self-portraits or Monet's water lilies). All these paintings look similar at first, and you have to analyze them closely to differentiate them. In my seminars I use slides of *The Lady and the Unicorn,* a series of six tapestries from fifteenth-century France. It is ideal for this exercise because of its rich motifs: the lady, the unicorn, and the flora and fauna of France in the middle ages. The theme of the five senses is ingeniously represented; you differentiate them by identifying details representing each sense, e.g., a mirror for sight. You can see it in Paris at the Musée de Cluny or find it in a book.

Exercise 1: Common Points and Differences

Analyze several pictures from the series, first looking for common points. Proceed systematically from the whole to the details. Then go over it once again, looking for differences. Comment on both and draw your own conclusions.

Exercise 2: Sensory Awareness and Observation

Include as many sensory modes as are relevant to the subject matter for each of the following items.

1. **Fruits:** Choose a fruit and analyze it by following the outline in this chapter. Do the same with other fruits from the same family and compare, considering what they have in common and what is specific to each one. Here are examples of types of fruit:

   Pears: Bartlett, Anjou, Bosc, Winter Nelis, Comice

   Apples: McIntosh, Pippin, Golden Delicious, Rome, Granny Smith

   Citrus: navel orange, tangelo, tangerine

2. **Flowers and plants:** Do the same with flowers and plants of your choice. Study different roses, tulips, wisterias, fuchsias, bougainvilleas, orchids, pansies, daisies, succulents, cacti, and ferns.

3. **Trees:** Study
   - The general shape and structure
   - The bark
   - The leaves
   - The fruit, if any
4. **Animals:** different cats, dogs, and birds.
5. **Miscellaneous objects:** e.g., lamps, garments.
6. **Posters,** billboards, magazine ads of particular products, e.g., watches, cars, beverages.
7. **Physical surroundings,** e.g., streets, parks, shopping centers, stores.
8. **People:** Observe faces, voices, posture, nervous habits, patterns of speech, etc.
9. **Music:** You can teach yourself how to listen better by analyzing the pieces of music you enjoy. For instance, take a song on a record or tape you like and *raise questions.*

   - Who is the singer? How could you characterize the singer's voice? Is it mellow or raucous? What is its range? Is it mostly made up of high tones or low tones? What is the singer's style? Is it casual, conversational, without frills, or is it stilted, stylized, romantic, ironic, lyrical? Is the singer trying to make a statement? What kind of lyrics does he or she use?
   - What about the instruments? Which ones are used? Analyze the quality of their sound. (For example, the saxophone usually has a sensuous quality, while the flute is often cheerful and impish.)
   - How is the rhythm? Fast or slow? Simple or complex? Can you easily follow the beat? Does it make you feel like dancing or like lounging?
   - What mood does the music convey?

- Try to follow separately melody and accompaniment in the two speakers of your stereo.

10. **Cheeses and wines:** Develop your taste buds by tasting and analyzing different cheeses. Start with the mildest and finish with the strongest. Try cheese with red wine and see how flavors complement each other. If you want to increase your appreciation of wines, taste several wines along the same principles: Start with the light and proceed to the full-bodied. Analyze them individually and compare them for better appreciation. Try different wines with different foods and watch for complementary tastes.

Exercise 3:   Differences in Details

Imagine you are decorating your house, shopping for furniture, e.g., compare chairs from the same manufacturer: similar chairs and different chairs. Proceed from general to detail, from size, line, proportions, comfort, to details in shape of legs, back, construction, etc.

PART 3

Improving Organization

CHAPTER 8

Association Techniques

*"The mind of man is more intuitive than logical,
and comprehends more than it can coordinate."*

Vauvenargues (1746)

Webster's New Collegiate Dictionary defines "association" as "the process of forming mental connections or bonds between sensations, ideas, or memories." There is a constant flow of unconscious associations at play in the mind as one reacts to all kinds of stimuli. Associations are very important in the learning process. One thing leads to another, and associations help organize the new material in many different ways. Depending on how we form associations, we can facilitate recall or make it more difficult. Psychologists Morris N. Young and Walter B. Gibson, following the general theory of natural and artificial memory, point out that "in natural memory, associations are logical . . . if natural and logical associations fail, those of an unnatural, illogical type can be introduced as artificial aids." This is the basis of mnemonics, or artificial aids to prompt recall.

Usually associations bring back memories effortlessly. This process is called involuntary memory. Something—a sound, a taste, a detail we see—triggers a memory. Usually we are reminded of a resemblance or a difference. When we meet someone, we look for common interests. When reading a book of fiction, we notice elements common to this type of writing: subject or theme, story line, characters, and plot. We may be reminded of a particular character in another novel we have read or a similar situation in our own lives. Great literature touches us individually. We both enjoy the fantasy and relate to the story personally. We all have a bit of Romeo and Juliet in us, not only because we fall in love but because we are frustrated by the way society and our families raise obstacles to our wishes. Most people perceive first what they have in common with the characters. Literary critics, film critics, and critically minded people search for what's original, that is to say, what's different. They try to define the "style" of an artist or writer as he or she expresses in a special, individual way feelings and ideas that are common to all people. For instance, Charlie Chaplin and Buster Keaton have their own ways of expressing sorrow and joy. They touch each of us differently.

Creative people always look for associations. Their minds are highly active, and they use the first associations as a springboard for more. The French poet Valéry wrote a pioneer essay on creativity in order to demystify the idea of "inspiration." Inspiration is the first association which enters the mind of the poet unexpectedly and without effort. It is only the starting point for the poem, however. If the poet does not search for more associations, he or she will have only one beautiful verse, not a poem. Craft (or technical know-how) turns ideas into art. It involves looking for interesting associations and creating original metaphors (images), rhymes, rhythms, and so forth.

Associations have interested philosophers for centuries. Aristotle, the founder of "associationism," was the first to divide them into voluntary and involuntary associations. In the eighteenth century, David Hume noticed that people have no control over involuntary associations since such associations depend on exterior *coincidence*. You don't plan to stumble on an uneven pavement, but as you do, this may trigger an association, or a recognition of a similar sensation felt long ago in another specific place.

At the turn of the century, Ebbinghaus spent his life analyzing associations, especially associations by "contiguity," that is, in a sequence. We shall come back to them a little later. More recently, Carl Jung carefully studied associations in people's dreams. In psychoanalysis people are asked to free-associate in order to recall memories which have been censored and buried in the unconscious.

As A. Leontiev points out in *The Development of Memory*, when we say, "Something reminded me of . . ." we acknowledge that an association came first and triggered our thinking. On the other hand, when we say, "I remembered," a thought came first and triggered associations. In the first case our thought follows an involuntary association. In the second case we think and search for associations in a voluntary, conscious manner.

It is interesting to identify the different kinds of associations. The ones which are given to us freely, by coincidence, are unpredictable. It may be a phonetic association, a sound that reminds us of another sound which has quite another meaning in another context or in another language. For example, *gâteau* ("cake" in French) sounds close to *gato* ("cat" in Spanish), which led a 5-year-old French girl to exclaim: "Maria (the Spanish baby-sitter) is crazy! She shows me a cat and says it's a cookie."

Some associations are easy to retrace because of contiguity. They rely on cause and effect. They are common to everyone, and you can trace them back through logical associations. Ivanov gives the example of Sherlock Holmes, who tries to guess what his friend Watson has been thinking. He retraces a chain of associations by contiguity, with one idea leading to the next within the context of the particular situation. Since the situation is precise and limited, so are the possibilities for associations. When you try to solve a mystery, you look for logical links (motive, opportunity, skill). When you are talking with someone about a subject you have both been thinking about, you may come up with the same associations, thus experiencing a feeling of telepathy: "Oh! that's just what I was thinking. How strange!" But it is not that strange, as Ivanov points out. These associations are quite different from the spontaneous ones mentioned earlier.

Since association reinforces memory at the unconscious level, it is reasonable to assume that it can do so at the conscious level. In other words, if we make conscious associations, if we look for them for specific reasons, we gain control over the recording of our memories. We also improve our chances of recall by reinforcing the mental connections. Weaving associations into a wide network, we enlarge the context, thus increasing the chances of hitting more cues and stirring more memories. Organizing associations is the key to efficient retention. Searching for associations or just becoming aware of them will become a game. Play the game and your memory will improve.

The basic methods of analysis and association can be applied to list learning. It is an easy way to measure your memory, as psychologists have known for years. List learning can be a memory feat illustrating the techniques and how they work, or it can be a practical way of managing in everyday life. We want to be able to function in everyday life without lists written on scraps of paper which eventually get lost or are forgotten. You will still make lists but will depend much less on them. Keep them in your pocket as a backup and a way to check your memory. By relying too much on notes or lists you fail to use your memory.

To fix the memory of a list, we analyze the elements in the list and make useful associations. When we analyze an object, we can look at it from several different angles.

1. *Analogical thinking* stresses the resemblances between objects. "Analogy" means "resemblance established by the *imagination* between two or several objects of essentially different character or meaning." An example might be, "She reminds me of my sister Sue because they both have blue eyes."

2. *Differential thinking* stresses the differences between compared items, even to include oppositions. An example might be, "I can remember Mr. Black's name because his hair is so white."

3. *Categorical thinking* puts items or ideas into categories. "Grouping" is the natural way of organizing thoughts, and "pairing" is the simplest of all. Shoe and sock, glass and bottle go together.

All these modes of thinking are complementary and can be used together for better retention. Kenneth Highbee reports that studies have shown an increase from 19 percent recall of lists to 65 percent when categories are used. Any category or association is better than none. More organization guarantees a higher recall rate. As we think about associations, we can also use visualization at a conscious level, which makes it even more effective. For instance, here is a list of things to do:

Mail letter

Go to the bank

Go to the hairdresser

Sharpen scissors

The items can be paired as follows: Mail letter and bank (there is a mailbox in front of the bank); hairdresser and scissors (hairdresser needs scissors to cut hair).

Grouping forces you to make an association; image association will make you visualize the association. Finally, using your imagination, you can reinforce your association even further.

Letter and bank: Imagine that you throw your checkbook in the mailbox and hand your letter to the bank clerk. This tragicomic image associates bank and letter while separating two operations. The analogy lies in the geographic proximity of the two.

Hairdresser and scissors: Imagine your hairdresser cutting your hair with your dull scissors. What a painful image!

With practice, searching for an association will become second nature. Grouping, counting items, and looking for image associations between them with the help of analogies, differences, opposites, and your imagination makes it easy to remember lists.

The principle of image association can be practiced in the following way. At the time of recording, first zoom in on the item to be remembered (e.g., your keys). Second, visualize it next to the object where you place it (e.g., near the telephone). Third, comment on how it fits there. At the time of recall, your keys and the phone will spring back to you as a single image. We spontaneously do that when we remember where we put something. We can "see it there." Doing it consciously will ensure that you won't forget as often.

Categories and General Principles

Searching for categories will help you remember instructions, recipes, and other procedures. Understanding the principle is the key to efficient learning. For example, cooking can be a pleasure once you understand the basic principles of food preparation. To remember how to prepare a sorrel sauce, think about the different types of sauces: white, brown, cream-based, and demiglace. In which category does your sorrel sauce fit? Think about the principle behind a white sauce. It starts with a roux of flour and butter mixed on the stove until bubbly and golden (a sign that the flour is cooked). Some kind of white liquid is added to this thickening agent. Here it is fish stock, as the sauce will complement salmon. Cream is added for smoothness at the last minute, when the sauce has been reduced to the consistency you desire. If you think about your new recipe with principles and categories in mind, you will only have to learn the different ingredients or the slight variations of procedures. For example, the flavorings are added to sauces in the last part of the cooking to retain maximum flavor. Here, add sherry and shredded sorrel leaves and simmer for a few minutes. Remove from the stove, add cream, and season to taste with salt and pepper.

The art of substituting ingredients for health or taste reasons relies on using the principles behind individual recipes. You can cut down on fat in two different ways, by using a nonstick pan and reduced broth or using a small quantity of margarine. Another example is remembering how knots are tied. Once I watched a demonstration of Tahitian pareu wear. The pareu, a rectangular piece of light cotton cloth, can be wrapped around the body in as many as 50 different ways. But few people remember more than three styles, the model told me. I set out to do better by looking for a few principles underlying all these variations. Three main principles stood out:

1. You can tie the corners together or you can create new ends by holding the material a few inches inside, letting the corners drop. (This reduces the amount of material passing through the knot.)

2. You can tie the pareu on the front, back, either side, over or under the shoulder, around the neck or above the breast.

3. You can cross toward the back or the front. If you have a very long pareu, you can pass the bottom part between the legs and tie it where you want: waist, hips, or breast.

This way anybody can reconstitute many more than three styles. Think in terms of general principles, or categories, and you will only have to remember the differences, i.e., the variations from the norm.

Trial Exercise

Recording Information

Here is a shopping list of 10 words, some of which we have already mentioned. Write it down vertically: cobbler, nuts, bread, bank, asparagus, hairdresser, lettuce, scissors, bananas, and mail.

1. Group the items as you wish into categories, such as supermarket items. Count the items in each category and analyze them, e.g., greens and fruits, nuts and bread.

2. Associate the items with a story. For instance, "banana nut bread" as a single image links three out of five supermarket items. This process improves your recall be-

cause you are obliged to tie the previously unrelated items together into a single neat package.

3. Check to see how many words you have remembered and try to make image associations with the ones you missed.

Conclusion

If we combine different kinds of associations and visualization, we have a very powerful tool with which to improve memory. Image association and imagination build a context necessary for good retention. As the philosopher David Hume used to say, association is "a gentle force" you can learn to master.

Quick Review

1. Associations bring back memories effortlessly.
2. Looking for specific associations—resemblances, differences, categories—helps you record and recall information.
3. Image association combines visualization and elaborate thought processes.
4. Imagination refines the process and personalizes your memories for better recall.
5. Thinking about general principles makes learning easy.

Exercises

Exercise 1: Images and Context

Figure 8-1 shows a set of objects. Try to categorize these objects into groups. Count them and make associations between items within each group. After 5 minutes take a piece of paper and write down the objects as you remember them. See how you organized the material.

Figure 8-1

Exercise 2:   Lists and Context

Try to group the following words in a way that will make memorizing easy for you. Invent a story linking them together and visualize the scene. Use your imagination.

Panda	Air
Carriage	Fern
Bee	Cat
Marigold	Sun
Daisies	Water

Exercise 3:   Visualization, Context, and Associations

For 2 minutes look at Figure 8-2, which contains the names of animals. Visualize them where they are and weave a story to associate them. Turn the page, take a piece of paper, and try to replace them exactly where they were originally.

Exercise 4:   Grouping and Associations

For 3 minutes look at a page of stamps from the National Wild Federation (or a similar series). Group them in such a way as to facilitate recall. See how many you remember.

Exercise 5:   Associations

This exercise will set your mind thinking about associations, which is one of the goals in improving the recording of memories. First write down all the associations which come to your mind from the following words:

Camel	Nail
Paris	Glass
Solar	Ring

Now try to analyze your associations. Classify them in different categories. (Reread the beginning of this chapter.) Continue thinking about associations all through the day and jot them down in your notebook.

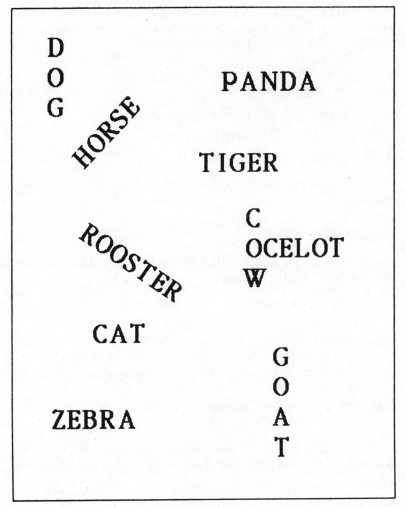

Figure 8-2

Exercise 6:   Grouping and Nonlogical
Associations

Make associations among the group of words on each line.
Look at the words and see if they remind you of something.
Write down the first free association that comes to mind. Let

your mind wander freely without restricting yourself to logical associations. You will end up making a ministory or building a picture on the screen of your mind.

1. book / flower / pastrami / soap
2. god / winter / paper / sad
3. chair / candle / slippery / mother
4. cat / trash / Monday / soccer
5. Kodak / river / plant / mysterious

For more practice, make up your own list, choosing words at random.

Exercise 7: Pairs

Write down the association which comes to your mind when you consider the following pairs of words.

1. tulip / umbrella
2. cat / shoes
3. candy / sorrow
4. painting / knife
5. sky / car
6. bush / berry
7. stick / leather
8. president / basket
9. water lily / chemistry
10. cloud / happy

Exercise 8: Transforming Abstract into Concrete

Find a concrete image association for each of the following abstract words. For example: Paris = the Eiffel Tower, love = a heart.

1. Winter
2. Poverty
3. Rock'n'roll
4. Heat
5. Liberty
6. Waltz
7. Dirt
8. Justice
9. Time
10. Death
11. Patience
12. Meal
13. Sickness
14. Energy
15. Politics
16. Speed

17. Hope   19. Tenderness
18. Greed   20. Happiness

Exercise 9:   Association and Visualization

Combining the following words, make a story and visualize it: duck, gold, charming, foot, primrose, knot.

Exercise 10:   Association and Visualization

Try to remember all the following names of flowers. Visualize them and associate them with one another. Make up a story to put them all in a context. Think of an imaginary garden, perhaps—be a landscape architect. Or you may want to compose a bouquet or several ones to give to different persons. Make a clear mental picture of the flowers all together. Review your associations. When you think you know them, set your kitchen timer to 5 minutes. When it rings, write down everything you remember: story, associations, and of course names of flowers.

Violet	Iris	Gladiola	Daisy
Orchid	Crocus	Wisteria	Tulip
Dahlia	Jasmine	Forget-me-not	Rose

NOTE   If you are eager to test yourself, try remembering these flowers for 2 or more days. You will be impressed how well this method works. If you are scientifically inclined, you may want to learn another list of flowers just through rote repetition, without associations or visualization, to see if you remember it as easily and accurately. You might also compare your results with the test you took at the beginning of the book. Do you find it easier to learn a list using associations?

Exercise 11:   Image Association

Advertising   Try to remember the images representing ads of products you've seen on television recently. Write down the

names of those products and visualize the ads. Write everything you see in your mind's eye, along with the memories it
triggers (voice, music, dialogue, scenery). By studying the ads
you remember better, you can learn a lot about how image
association helps memory. The product and its name must be
closely associated in a single striking image, placing it in its
context. If you think "clean and fresh" when you visualize
Irish Spring soap and the Irish girl in the grass "fresh as a
whistle," the ad worked. Same if you think "soft skin and hair"
and visualize Mink soap and hair spray ads.

Name Brands   Here is a list of products often seen adver-
tised on TV, billboards, and magazines. Visualize the ad (image
association) and describe it briefly in as much detail as you can.

1. Calvin Klein jeans	9. Bank services
2. Oil of Olay	10. Car sales
3. Tareyton cigarettes	11. Carpet sales
4. Federal Express	12. Computers
5. American Express	13. Bell Telephone
6. Hanes Hosiery	14. Gasoline
7. Toilet paper	15. Stores
8. Over-the-counter drugs	

TIP TO PROMPT RECALL   Try fishing for cues. It is a guess-
ing game which prompts easy recall through recognition: the
trick is to ask questions, hoping that one will hit the cue. It
works as an insurance policy against weak or nonexistent image
association. Instead of waiting for cues to come to you, actively
search for them. Ask general questions, then more specific ones
determined by the context. (It should be about time, place,
mood, topic, people, etc.) These principles can be applied to
anything you may want to recall. *Call* the questions and you will
recall.

Exercise 12:   Paired Associates and Nonlogical Associations

This exercise will consist of visualizing two ill-matched objects together. Try not to resist the strange association but rather have fun with it simply because *it works.*

1. Make a clear mental image of each object.
2. Now visualize the two objects together until you come up with one clear image association of the two together.

In the process you will become aware of your thoughts and emotions as you start weaving a ministory association. Let all associations come through; do not try to censor them. For example, use the words "hair" and "water." Imagine a beautiful hairdo destroyed by a sudden rainfall or Ophelia's hair floating among water lilies. Each person will have his or her own association. Choose the first one that comes to your mind. Make your image association dramatic if you can: Emotions of humor, joy, sorrow, anger, or surprise will help you process it more deeply. Here are 10 pairs to use in your ministories. Visualize each pair together.

1. pot / corridor
2. carpet / coffee
3. earring / lamp
4. palm tree / chewing gum
5. dentist / bathroom

6. sun / fingers
7. patio / scissors
8. steak / sand
9. nail / dictionary
10. unicorn / coat

Now that you have accepted the principle of artificial, nonlogical associations, you are ready to learn memory systems based on this kind of image association.

CHAPTER 9

Memorizing Names and Faces

*"Our names are the light that glows on the sea
waves at night and then dies without leaving its
signature."*

Rabindranath Tagore (1906)

We live in a society which stresses the importance of the individual. Hence, we have to remember faces and names in order to function and feel integrated into our social and working environment. Unlike the Europeans, we cannot get away with a polite "Good morning, madam" with no name attached. The more familiar "dear" fills the gap but leaves us a bit ashamed and dissatisfied. As we get older, names seem to elude us more often. We wait anxiously for words to come back, and often they don't.

Although we may be bad at remembering names and faces, we do remember some of them, and it is worthwhile trying to understand how we usually do it without being aware of it. In everyday life we remember the names of people we deal with all the time. Reviewing the name and seeing the person often keeps it up front in one's consciousness. We may hear others say the name or read it on letters, mailboxes, desks, or doors. All of these act as reminders or prompters. However, few people remember the name of a person they seldom see or have just met. Those who do have *extra motivation*. They show genuine interest in names and derive great satisfaction from performing the feat of remembering them. They practice this skill all the time, making spontaneous associations. Above all they make it a point to remember names, whereas most people give up and stop trying. Some automatic associations help recall. When they fit, we do remember. For instance, if a graceful girl is named Grace, you may notice the connection, and her graceful features will be spelled out in your mind as "Grace." The same thing may happen if the person you have just met has the same name as a friend of yours, especially if they look somewhat alike. The mind stretches to find associations in a quite natural way. The names we tend to remember somehow ring a bell. They are more concrete because we link them to some meaning. Too often, we leave this process to chance and to spontaneous logical associations. An overall poor record can be drastically improved by learning how to associate face and name by means of an artificial association.

The following method is based on image association. You are already familiar with the principle. You use it when you attach a concrete image association to a name to help you remember it: Ford like the car company or Levi like Levi's jeans. But most people do not carry this association a step further, to the face, and therefore it stays in the mind in the little compartment where "names" are kept, disconnected from "faces." It is easy to visualize a face when given a name. However, putting a name on a face is the real challenge. If you are willing to use your new motivation skills and your imagination, you will find it easy to use the following method to plant a cue from the name onto the face. Next time you see the face, it will contain a visual cue to the name.

To associate a name with a face, we must become aware of what is striking in the face as well as in the name. Analyzing the face, we will look for the dominant feature; analyzing the name, we will look for a concrete image, a concrete meaning through a name transformation. Finally, we will associate both dominant feature and name transformation together in a single image association. These three steps require a certain amount of time, which should decrease with practice. Thus, do not feel hurried when you are working on your association. It is the essential step which will enable you to connect the name to the face of the person you want to remember.

Faces are more easily remembered than names because they form concrete images. If you want to put a name on a face, you must extract a concrete meaning from the name. This search should lead you to an image which you can visualize and associate with the face. Unless you make a conscious effort to link name to face, you will remember them separately and not necessarily at will.

Before you start, look carefully at the face and listen carefully to the name. (Most of the time we don't pay attention.) Then enjoy making your image association. Use your imagination when looking for name transformations and while visualizing the association.

To select the dominant feature, you will find it easier to start by looking at the face in a candid way and become aware of how you perceive it. Be sensitive to the way it affects you and try to see how specific features touch you. Note your reactions. For instance, greasy hair, gentle smile, radiant skin—think how you would feel if you touched it. This may lead you directly to what strikes you in the face: the dominant feature. Then ask yourself which in your opinion is the most striking feature. One may jump out at you immediately, but if not (which is most often the case), proceed by analyzing every feature, one after another, in a systematic manner: shape of face, hair, forehead, eyes, nose, cheeks, mouth, chin, skin. Notice the specific details. Ask yourself which among these features you find most striking: You may have spent more time analyzing it and may have made some comments about it. Once you have selected the dominant feature, zoom in on it.

The Dominant Feature

Since the face is the stimulus which leads back to the name, first become aware of the feature which strikes you most. (This is a subjective approach—it is your opinion that counts. Do not try to find the objective feature that everyone would agree on, since this is seldom possible.) The feature that strikes you most is the dominant feature. Concentrating on it will strengthen the stimulus leading to recognition. Next time you see the face, the dominant feature will strike you again provided that you have analyzed its characteristics and made a point to visualize it at length. It probably would have struck you unconsciously, but what you are doing here is making sure that it does by isolating and analyzing it. You are reinforcing your memory while reinforcing the exterior stimulus. (The more precise, the better.) Then close your eyes and see if you can recreate the dominant feature in your mind. Try to see it in the context of the face. Do you have a clear image? If not, check again.

NOTE   It is important to select one dominant feature. If you cannot decide between two, choose one *arbitrarily*. This will go faster if you try to be receptive to what strikes you. Look for the most interesting, striking, different, unusual feature. Once you have identified one dominant feature, stick to it and go on analyzing it and visualizing it. Do not switch from one feature to another. Rather, focus your attention on the one you have selected. You will replace it in its context, the whole face, quite naturally by mere observation: While looking at the dominant feature, you cannot help seeing the rest of the face. Learn to select one item and concentrate on it because a specific image is easier to visualize than a nonspecific one.

Name Transformation

From now on, look for *meaning* in names. Your goal is to find a concrete meaning to the name. We call this the *name transformation*. The abstract name should become concrete; this is more or less difficult according to the name. Say the name aloud to yourself and listen carefully. Does it sound like a word you know or like a combination of two words? You will soon get into the habit of reading a meaning into names. You must choose a meaning you can visualize. This new perspective will provide you with a concrete image for each name.

Some names lend themselves to direct transformations; the concrete meaning is built in. For instance, the names Sterling, Carpenter, and Mann:

Sterling = sterling silver   Carpenter = a carpenter
Mann = a man

In these cases you just need to think about the meaning of the name and use it to make a clear image illustrating this meaning. People seldom pay attention to the meaning of names because many names have none or have been distorted or because it does not seem to be relevant. (In the old days, in less complex societies, names corresponded to points of reference which were useful. For instance, Baker was the baker and Carpenter was the carpenter. Names had a concrete meaning and were easily remembered in their context.) Other names will require some work and the help of your imagination. Repeat the name *aloud* to yourself until it rings a bell, and the meaning will stem from a sound association with another word. Phonetic (sound) approximation is quite satisfactory for memory purposes as long as it includes a concrete image. For instance, Klein sounds like "climb"; Barclay is easily transformed into "bar of clay," just as Westphal is into "west fall." These direct or indirect name transformations provide a concrete image corresponding to the name. We end up with two clear images that we can "visualize" as one: (1) the dominant feature and (2) the name transformation. The last and most important step consists of combining the two in a single image association.

NOTE With some names you may find yourself short of ideas and therefore be frustrated, but do not give up on this technique before having tried it for some time. With practice, you will develop the ability to find a meaning in every name. (It is like stretching your muscles: When you start a fitness program the goal seems impossible to reach, yet by doing the exercises you will progress.)

Image Association

To bring the two concrete images together, *arbitrarily* place the concrete image extracted from the name transformation onto the dominant feature. Then visualize this composite image until you know it well. In Chapter 8, "Association Techniques," you learned how to make image associations of two unrelated objects. Now you can see the practical application: Literally, you put a name (or something that stands for it) on a face.

Commenting on the Image Association

Commenting on the image association engraves it even better in your memory. Making a judgment of how your name transformation fits the prominent feature strengthens the association. Play with the illogical rather than rebel against it.

In order to fix the association in your memory, it is mandatory to spend some time visualizing the two images into a single one (15 seconds at least). For example:

Dr. YESAVAGE: Dominant feature: EYEBROWS

Name transformation: YES SAVAGE (indirect)

Image association: Place a symbol for SAVAGE (e.g., headband of feathers) on his eyebrows.

Visualize primitive tribal ritual feathers on his eyebrows. You must be able to describe accurately the dominant feature (dark, bushy, prominent). Otherwise, it could be somebody else's. Say the name Yesavage while visualizing feathers on his eyebrows. Make sure you link SAVAGE to FEATHERS; otherwise you may end up saying, "Hello, Doctor Duck." Visualize feathers but think and say, "Savage, yes savage, Yesavage."

Sometimes one is lucky and the first association that pops

into one's head matches the situation. Here, for instance, I thought of the caveman, who had a prominent forehead with bushy eyebrows and deeply set eyes. This image association is perfectly adequate. Cavemen = prominent eyebrows = savage. However, you must be aware of one thing: It is easy to project an image from the name that is not clearly there on the face. Suppose a woman named Hartley has a face with a pointed chin. You find her mouth unusual and a perfect dominant feature. As you start searching for a name transformation, you come up with "heart." Suddenly her face with its pointed chin looks to you heart-shaped. You are tempted to change your choice of dominant feature and abandon the image association altogether, saying, "Oh, that's easy! It's obvious!" However, although it may be obvious now, it will not be so next time you see the woman. Why? Simply because it is the name that triggered the association, not vice versa. You need a stronger cue, an *objective* cue which you place there artificially so that it brings back the name. You do not want a vague projection. Next time you see the face, it may not strike you as heart-shaped. (It had not before you thought "heart"). Do not try to match cue and feature.

Artificially placing an object on a feature is a sure way to record an efficient image association. You leave no room for subjective projection of the kind just mentioned. If it comes to you, accept it as a bonus but continue applying the mnemonic. It really pays off, because it is designed to trigger recall. If you place a string of flying hearts coming out of her mouth, next time you see that face, you will zoom in on the mouth and will see a string of hearts built into the image. "Heart" will remind you of Hartley. This method has proved very effective in my memory classes. There I have the opportunity to teach it with slides. The demonstration is impressive. After being coached with 12 pictures, people remember the names when shown the faces. I ask: "What is the prominent feature? What did we put on it, i.e., what name transformation? What is the name?" And all are amazed at how easily the chain of recall flows from the stimulus (feature) to the cue (name transformation) to the name.

Helpful Points for Doing Faces and Names Exercises

Faces

To get a better image of the face, look for specific information about each feature before deciding on a dominant feature. Proceed from hair to chin. For example, consider the following.

Hair: Look at volume, color, texture, hairline, and length. Is it curly, straight, or wavy? Coarse or fine? Oily or dry?

Nose: Consider the size, the width, the distance from tip to upper lip. Focus on the nostrils; like fingerprints, they are all different.

Mouth: Note the size and shape. Also look at the teeth, lips, and smile.

General impression: Is the face angular or round? Soft or hard?

An accurate study of features will prevent you from misidentifying them at the time of recognition.

Names

You might produce a mental file of categories of names with a visual symbol attached. For example, consider the following.

Occupational names: Carpenter = hammer or saw; Singer = your favorite pop star.

Names of things: Forest, Church = visualize a particular one

Names of places: Berlin = the wall

Brand names and famous names: Campbell = soup; Carter = a cart full of peanuts at the White House

Remember that all the associations which come to your mind are precious for memory. Think of them as a bonus. However, the visual ones for which you are searching are special. They are meant to trigger recall, to cue you when you need help. Continue looking for name transformations and make image associations between items you can visualize.

Image Associations

Since active images are remembered better, add movement to your images; e.g., visualize gluing feathers on Dr. Yesavage's eyebrows against the wind.

Ridiculous images are not easier to remember, contrary to what some people have said. What is mandatory is to make a clear image association.

If you remember the dominant feature but not immediately what you placed on it, go over the feature again. As you analyze it in detail, all the comments you made about it will come back. As we have seen, weaving a little story with personal associations is a sure way to strengthen the link. For instance, you may have said for Mrs. Stover, who has a big mouth, "A stove may well fit into it if I pass it through this wider corner." This remark will come back when you notice how large her mouth is. Integrating the particular details of the feature is the key to a strong association. Use your imagination. Once you have the name transformation, you have your cue to the person's name.

At this point, even if you cannot retrieve the real name, you will be so close that you should not worry: Go ahead and say Mrs. Window instead of Mrs. Windor, Mr. Wrestle instead of Mr. Russell, Miss Adam instead of Miss Adams. It sounds so close that people may not notice the name transformation. If they do, they will correct you, and next time you'll get it right. To be 80 percent right is better than nothing. For best results in a social situation, ask the name of the person before parting, immediately look for a name transformation, and then go to another room and visualize the cue on a feature you found striking while talking to the person.

First Names and Names of Miscellaneous Things

Get into the habit of searching for meaning in a name. Then translate this meaning into an image symbol. Here is an example of useful image association to remember names other than family names. You can use this method for names of books, movie titles, brand names of products, streets, and so on.

Suppose you want to remember the name of a man who comes to repair your refrigerator. It may help just to make an association between the item to be repaired (the refrigerator) and the name of the man (say it is Alfredo). Alfredo reminds you of a friend called Alfred. Associate the three together: your friend, Alfredo, and the refrigerator. Visualize your friend inspecting the refrigerator. Next time you think "broken refrigerator," you will see Alfred, which will remind you of Alfredo, a Spanish or Italian version of your friend's name.

If you have another association, use it. For instance, you may have thought of fettuccini Alfredo. Visualize this Italian dish filling up your refrigerator. When you think "refrigerator," you will see the pasta everywhere, which will cue you to the name Alfredo. Another association which comes to my mind stems from Italian: *al freddo* = "in the cold." This association fits the context of the refrigerator. I would make a note of it and visualize the repairperson screaming in Italian because he is locked inside *"al freddo."*

There are millions of possible associations. You will find that they come easily once you start looking for them. Make it a game! Train yourself to remember names by asking the name of anyone who helps you. In restaurants, stores, banks, and post offices, you often just have to look at name tags. When you watch a movie, try to get the names of the main characters.

Some people remember names without this method. How do they do it? Motivation, concentration, a mental operation of some kind to imprint the message, and constant practice. In one of my classes there was a woman who managed to remember the first and last names of the 12 people whose pictures I showed as a pretest. This was so unusual as to be suspicious, but there was no way she could have cheated. When I asked her how she did it, she could not explain her technique other than by mentioning associations and fixed places. But she said she had been a schoolteacher for 35 years and always made it a point to remember the names of all her students the first day of class. Why set herself such a difficult goal? She explained that it was her way of gaining immediate control over her class: "I never had any problems with discipline. A child called upon by his name right away got the message he was being watched personally." The magic worked for both the student and the teacher's memory. Few people have such high motivation, however, which is why most of us benefit from memory systems. Recall is so much easier when we use them. See for yourself.

Quick Review

To put a name on a face, it is necessary to identify one dominant feature of the face, concretize the name (name transformation), and artificially place the image extracted from the name onto the dominant feature. This specific method of image association guarantees good recording and good recall in every case (and not only when the name matches the face; e.g., Miss Piggy has a snouty nose like a pig).

At the time of recording, make sure you do the three steps in the following order.

1. *Face:* Look for *one dominant feature* (striking, different, unusual).

2. *Name:* Listen for a *name transformation* ("Does the name mean anything?").

3. *Image association:* Visualize the two together for 15 seconds. Use your imagination and have fun with the nonlogical association. Accepting the artificiality of the system is the key to success.

To reinforce the memory trace, make an affective judgment about the image association, commenting on how the name transformation fits the dominant feature. You will be able to retrieve the cue (name transformation) by simply reviewing the feature: All your remarks will spring back to you. To retrieve the name, just retrace the steps of the chain of associations from the stimulus back to the name.

At the time of recall, ask yourself these questions.

1. What is the *dominant feature?*
2. What did I put on it? (*name transformation*)
3. What is the *name?*

If you are unsuccessful, you probably have not concretely defined the dominant feature or the name transformation. You must have a clear image of both. It may also be that you have not spent enough time visualizing the two images together. Try *15 seconds to start with.* Increase your motivation by choosing to remember someone in whom you are really interested. Don't give up at your first frustration! Keep on trying, and you will succeed.

Exercises

Exercise 1:   Meeting People

1. When you meet someone for the first time, *look* at the person's face and determine its most striking feature. This is the dominant feature that will strike you first the next time you see this face.
2. *Listen* to the name and analyze it. Search for meaning in the name. Transform the abstract name into a concrete word that you will be able to visualize to make your image association.
3. *Associate* the name and the face, placing the image derived from the name transformation onto the dominant feature. Search for a story or a strong image associating the two. Visualize the two concrete objects together as a single image. Spend at least 15 seconds making your image association. This is the key to success in record-

ing what you want to remember. For better concentration, go to another room to make your association. And be confident. You can do it!

Exercise 2:　Study Pictures and Names

Figure 9-1 shows 12 pictures of people. Apply the method outlined in the preceding exercise, paying particular attention to the name transformation. Is it a direct transformation built into the name (such as Fox or Lyon)? Or is it one that requires your imagination (such as Yesavage = "yes savage")? Turn the page and see how many names you can remember (Figure 9-2).

Exercise 3:　Name Transformations

Write down the last names of 10 people you know. Look for meaning in each name until you find a name transformation you can visualize.

Exercise 4:　Visual Symbols for Name Transformations

You can prepare a list of visual symbols ready to use. For example, all names beginning with *Mc-* might be visualized with a shamrock in the background, whereas the prefix *Mac-* will translate into a tartan or bagpipes. Do the same with suffixes (*-son* or *-sen* might translate into "sun," etc.) Think of symbols for common names you often encounter, so that you will have them ready when you meet people with those names.

Exercise 5:　Differences among Faces

Train yourself to look for differences. Each day choose *one* face and analyze it feature by feature. Once you have isolated the dominant feature, look at it in detail. Suppose the dominant feature is the nose. You will then compare it with all the noses you see during the day. After a week, I am confident that you will be more aware of how different every individual feature is.

NOTE Don't worry if you cannot find the words to describe details at first. Just observe closely and make mental pictures of the differences.

Exercise 6: More Practice

Make it a game. Pick names and faces from any sources you wish: magazines, TV, or real people you happen to meet. In your notebook, write down the following for each: dominant feature, name transformation, image association, name. Make a real effort to apply the method. Drill, drill, drill.

Exercise 7: Remember Names of Other Things

To remember names of flowers, streets, products, book titles, or other objects, try to use the following principles.

1. Analyze the name and find a concrete transformation with meaning for you.

2. Repeat this meaningful name transformation as you look at the object.

3. Associate this name transformation with the object, visualizing the two together.

Train yourself at every opportunity. For example, as I was hiking one spring, I discovered a flower I had never seen before. I looked at it closely and found its name in my flower guidebook: Godetia. I looked for an association and came up with "Godiva," a brand of chocolate. I also realized that the French word for container is *godet*. As I repeated "Godetia" every time I saw the flower, I visualized a container of Godiva chocolate topped with these flowers. Since I had to remember the concept in French, I added the Eiffel Tower to my image association. It worked: I remember the name now whenever I see the flower. Similarly, when I learned of a new park called Butano, I thought of butane camping gas, which I imagined

1. Frances
   Ada

2. Javaid
   Sheikh

5. Robert
   Hill

6. Emily
   Gere

9. Kelvin
   Lim

10. Karen
    Evankovich

Figure 9-1

3. Jerome
    Yesavage

4. Gwen
    Yeo

7. Leslie
    Widrow

8. Elizabeth
    Tanke

11. Von
    Leirer

12. Paul
    Hicks

Figure 9-1 (cont.)

Figure 9-2

Figure 9-2 (cont.)

could keep me warm on the windy coast where the park is located. Try this when you come across new items.

Another example: I tried on a bathing suit in a shop in a small street in Cannes, France. I looked at the street sign— "rue Molière"—named after the famous French playwright. I had a meaning and a visual image, since I could visualize Molière's portrait. In addition, being familiar with his comedies, I imagined him making fun of women's vanity as they tried on bikinis. With his seventeenth-century curly wig, he looked quaint in the context of the shop. When I looked up for the name of the cross street and read "rue de la République," I just added a republican symbol to the scene. I will remember where the shop is for years to come, through image association.

Last example: Apply the same principle to remember the names of authors and their books, directors and their movies, and so forth. Colette Dowling wrote the *Cinderella Complex*. "Dowling" sounds like "scowling." I visualize Cinderella scowling as I repeat, "Colette Dowling, *Cinderella Complex*." Marcia Nasatir directed the movie *The Big Chill*. "Nasatir" sounds close to "Nagasaki," a place associated with a "big, chilling nuclear disaster." I visualize it while I say "Marcia Nasatir, *Big Chill*." You could also think "NASA" and "satyr," adding other associations.

Look for meaning in initials such as HDL (good) versus LDL (bad) cholesterol. If you are scientifically minded it will be easy to remember what these initials stand for, provided you can get that information. (I could not find it in the articles I read on the subject.) If you don't have a scientific background, just make up a meaning that will coincide with the positive or negative effect of the different substances. Here I notice the common letters DL. They happen to be my initials, but they could trigger "Dear Lord" in almost anyone. Assuming that H=high, and L=low, you must associate high with "high protection, high above danger." To remember which one is the good cholesterol you just need to remember "High Dear Lord." Looking for a context for L=low you could think "Low Dear Lord, I feel low with this diagnosis."

If within a few months all your efforts to remember names fail in social situations, ask yourself whether you really care. (I've noticed I remember names only when I really make it a point to do so.) If you are sure you do, try Frederick Skinner's sense of humor: When he must introduce his wife to someone whose name he has forgotten, he uses this strategy: "If there is any conceivable chance that she could have met the person, I simply say to her: -Of course you remember . . . ? and she grasps the outstretched hand and says: Yes of course, how are you? The acquaintance may not remember meeting my wife, but he is not sure of *his* memory either." This is not a copout. This is coping.

CHAPTER 10

First Things First: How to Remember a List in Order

" 'Begin at the beginning,' the King said, gravely, 'and go till you come to the end; then stop.' "

Lewis Carroll

In Chapter 8, "Association Techniques," you discovered how much easier it is to remember a list of items by grouping them into categories and weaving them together with a little story. Add to this what you now know about sensory awareness and visualization and you will be able to reinforce your memory by making a clear, concrete image of the items. Together, these mental operations can give you satisfactory results for most everyday lists. They are not foolproof, however. You may remember only part of the list unless you have a way to check and prompt yourself with preorganized thinking.

Mnemonics are systems of thought devised to increase control over recall. You are already familiar with the face and name mnemonic. You'll now learn an ancient mnemonic to remember a list in order. It may come in handy if you want to save gas, time, and money while running errands, or it may help you remember steps in procedures such as lighting the pilot of your furnace and cleaning the filter of your pool. You will discover other uses once you understand how it works. From personal challenge to social game it was popular for centuries before falling into disuse with the invention of the printing press.

160

Like faces and names, the loci mnemonic is a practical application of image association. Do you remember the last exercise in Chapter 8? It was called "Paired Associates," and you had to visualize two objects together in a single picture (for example, lamp and earring). That's what you were doing when you placed an object (symbolizing a name) on the dominant feature: You associated the two together in a single image. By now you should not find it strange to associate items which do not ordinarily belong together. You are going to apply the same principle to many areas. Some associations may seem silly, but so what, if they help you remember. You are alone in the privacy of your mind; unless you say something, nobody will know your associations.

People with extraordinary memories use image association spontaneously. If you read the accounts of the Russian mnemonist Shereshevskii by A. R. Luria in *The Mind of a Mnemonist,* you will enter a fantasy world that will amaze you. His mind is a screen; he thinks in images as easily as he breathes. You can develop the same technique. You may not become expert at it, but you will begin to feel more in control, taking in stride the normal forgetfulness that is part of the memory process. The poor Russian mnemonist suffered a great deal because he could not forget many insignificant details. Inability to select the essential was a handicap: Sometimes he could not see the forest for the trees. This explains why, although usually related through good organization, memory and intelligence are two separate things. Most intelligent people have good memories, but researchers have found that not all mnemonists have high IQs. Actually, memory, knowledge, practice, and techniques prove to be more important than IQ, especially since IQ only evaluates how well a person is likely to do in our school system.

There is a new trend in learning strategies which is very encouraging, especially for adults. Speed of thought is now considered less important than flexibility and openness to different options. Einstein was a slow thinker yet one of the most important ones. If you need to learn what is new in your field lest you lose ground, you had better use your memory more efficiently. In one episode of *A walk through the Twentieth Century,* Bill Moyers summed up our modern dilemma: "Never have so many people understood so little about so much." To keep up with progress and the flood of new information, you will have to be more efficient at learning. In the following chapters you will learn how, by using certain principles, you can devise your own systems of association. Here you will have your first opportunity to create your own reference file of image associations.

Memorizing a list in order is more difficult when you are dealing with unrelated items because it is often impossible to use logical groupings or analytical thinking to relate the items. Instead, you can rely on an artificial system based on fixed places, or *loci,* which will serve as reference points for images and associations made in connection with the items to be remembered. The idea is that you will not have to worry about the order. Your loci will be familiar places you can retrace spontaneously, and your list of items will follow that order.

Loci means "places" in Latin. The loci method was used by Roman orators to memorize the different parts of a speech. An orator would choose a familiar building, such as the Forum, setting aside a certain number of spots, or loci, one next to another. There he would "place" objects associated with his speech. For example, if the orator wanted to talk about war, he might place (in his imagination) a spear in the first place—the butcher's shop, perhaps. If the war was about food supplies, he might place a sack of grain in the second place—the cobbler's. He would continue in this fashion until he had placed every section of the speech. To present it, he would go through a mental tour, following the places in their natural order, and he would link the first statement to the first place, the second to the second place, and so on. This is how the classic opening line "In the first place . . ." came to be.

Each orator had his own logically ordered loci, which he always followed. The Roman orators found the method especially useful when they had to cover unrelated subjects, for analytical thinking helps people organize transitions only if there can be a logical link between the two elements. The loci method responds to a need for an artificial ordering quite apart from analytical thinking. You will probably find it easy to go through your house and, in a manner similar to that of the Romans, number the loci (in this case, rooms) from the entrance to the back of the house in an order which is natural to you. If your list is longer than your loci, just add a tour of each individual room. For example, the living room could be divided into a number of subdivisions: the carpet, the sofa, the fireplace, the stereo, and the television. Follow the same pattern in every room, always moving in the same direction, perhaps clockwise. Say you want to remember to run your errands in a certain sequence: Simply visualize each item and link it to each place. This will fasten the image association and trigger recall in the order you want.

ITEMS TO REMEMBER	LOCI
1. Garage	1. Entrance door
2. Bank	2. Corridor
3. Post office	3. Living room
4. Cleaner's	4. Dining room
5. Supermarket	5. Kitchen

On the one hand, you have the list of things to do and the sequence in which you should do them. On the other hand, you have the loci, the familiar places you will retrace at leisure in the given order.

1. Think about the first item to be remembered: the garage. Then make a mental image of your car blocking the front door and being stuck there because it needs to be repaired. Then ponder the association: garage–front door.

2. Do the same for all of the other items. For bank–corridor, imagine a teller smiling at you there or the floor covered with the checks you want to deposit.

3. Post office–living room: Imagine the parcel you need to mail waiting on your favorite armchair. (A specific ob-

ject in the room is easier to visualize than a whole room.)

4. Cleaner's–dining room: Imagine your clothes lying on the table, neatly packaged in the cleaner's plastic (or crumpled and dirty if you are taking them there).

5. Supermarket–kitchen: This one happens to be a logical association, so imagine your refrigerator empty or, on the contrary, overflowing with the food you need to buy (vegetables, milk, etc.).

To remember your list of errands in order, you only have to go over your loci, which you know well, and the associated items will pop out automatically. This does require some time and effort spent on visualizing your image association (specific items in specific places). You will have to use your imagination and visualize things in places where they normally do not belong. Rarely will you come across a logical association such as supermarket–kitchen, since you cannot choose to place items where you want. The order of your loci is preestablished, and the order of your list of things to remember has been determined by you. Neither should be changed to fit a logical association. Doing that would defeat the purpose of the system. Accept the strange associations as they happen and play with them. Just place the first item in the first place, the second item in the second place, and so on. Make sure you spend 15 seconds visualizing each item in the right place in order to seal your image association. Pay special attention to "easy" associations, for we tend to dismiss them too quickly. There is always a minimal amount of time needed to process information. *Don't assume you will remember. Make sure you will.*

You will keep a list in mind for about 24 hours. After that it will fade. The system works like a blackboard for rapid use, with the next list erasing the previous one. If for some reason you do not like using your house for your set of loci, there are alternatives. For example, you could use another building, a main street, a shopping center you know well, your bedroom, your car, or the pockets of a suit or purse. There are many possibilities. The main idea is to choose a permanent and familiar set of loci you can retrace in a fixed order.

Later on you may want to use several sets of loci to keep some permanent lists. For instance, you may use your kitchen only to itemize the contents of your safety deposit box. It may prove useful to keep in mind what you have there. Afterwards you may not worry as I did when I thought my pearl necklace had disappeared! Such lists will stay in your memory provided that you review them often.

The Loci Method

The loci method is based on image association; that is, you have to make a clear mental image of the item you want to remember and associate it with a certain place to which you can refer easily. In order to play the loci game, you must give up looking for logical associations. On the contrary, the system is based on *illogical* image associations.

First of all, you must decide on a set of places which are familiar to you. This is the most important step, and you should spend some time on it, making sure that you get a clear and *permanent* framework with which to work. You will need 20 loci to start with.

1.   Visualize or draw a map of your house, apartment, or room. Start at the entrance door and proceed through the room or rooms in the order that is natural to you. *Decide once and for all to go in a certain direction:* clockwise, for instance. You will always take your mental walk through your familiar loci in this order to make your image associations with the items you want to remember.

2.   Then name and number your loci, using a list as follows (these are my loci):
     1. Mailbox   3. Patio
     2. Entrance door   4. Glass door

5. Corridor	13. Shower
6. Living room	14. Study
7. TV room	15. Washer and dryer
8. Kitchen	16. Blue room
9. Dining room	17. Bathroom
10. Master bedroom	18. Yellow room
11. Walk-in closet	19. Garden
12. Sink	20. Garage

There are many places you can choose. In this example I did not detail the rooms because my house is large. If I lived in a studio apartment, I could have detailed it as follows: (1) mailbox, (2) entrance door, (3) corridor, (4) stereo, (5) leather chair, (6) tables and loudspeakers, (7) couch, (8) low table, (9) fireplace, (10) orange chair, (11) bookshelves, (12) TV set, (13) gray table, (14) chairs around, (15) painting above, (16) sofa bed, (17) nest of tables, (18) sculptured lamp, (19) wall clock, (20) carpet.

As you'll see, it is not difficult to find loci. You can detail as many rooms as you want. Experience has taught me to visualize *one* object as a symbol for a room which is not detailed: The more specific the image of the place, the easier it is to make an image association with the item to be remembered. For example, when I think "kitchen," the first (and dearest) object that comes to my mind is my refrigerator. It has the beautiful patina of old age and is more roomy than all the new ones I have seen. Choose your loci spontaneously, selecting objects you like best. Just make sure to take them in a natural order.

3. Now take a mental tour through your loci in the order and direction you have set up. Get a clear picture of each place and its number. You should be able to learn your selection of places rapidly, because you are following the natural layout of your house. Since your loci are permanent and familiar, you know them already and will visualize them in order when you need them.

As you reread your list, see if you can visualize each place clearly and distinctively. No place should be hard to picture. (One woman pointed out that she always missed the items she placed on a table hidden in the corner of a dark hall. If you cannot "see" a place clearly, skip it, because it will prove to be a weak spot.)

4. As soon as you have established your list of places, you will be ready to use the loci method for remembering a list in order. Read the following two sections first, however; they will make it easier for you.

Helpful Hints

1. *Do not try to speed up* the process of image association. With practice, you will do it faster, but it will always require some time: a few seconds at least. Memories are never recorded instantly. Time and effort are always involved for depth of processing, even if we are not conscious of it.

2. *Adding an emotional impression* to the image association deepens the recording of memories. It makes it more personal since it involves several aspects of your personality. For example:

ITEM	PLACE	IMAGE ASSOCIATION	EMOTION
bread	mailbox	It does not fit in.	What a pity to try to squeeze it in!

3. *Play with the irrational,* bizarre associations rather than fight them. You may at first resist the system on rational grounds ("This is silly.") But try it; it works!

4. *Be patient: Give yourself a chance.* It takes time to understand the system, accept it as a valuable tool, and finally apply it.

Mistakes to Avoid

1. *Avoid rushing to write your loci.* Take your time in establishing your permanent set of loci. *This is the most important step.* Select the places you want to visualize carefully; use the trial exercise to test them. If your loci are not clear and in a "natural" order, you will have difficulty retracing them. When you have a set of loci with which you are comfortable, write your permanent list in your notebook.

2. *Avoid choosing two similar loci* (for example, two end tables, two closets, two or more similar chairs). Group them as a single image. It is confusing to visualize the same thing in two different places, and your precious order is apt to be lost.

3. *Skip doors unless they are very special:* To avoid confusion, do not include inside doors: They are too neutral and similar. As if you were a ghost, ignore the doors of all those rooms.

4. *Choose permanent loci.* Do not choose objects which change places. Books do, for instance, unless it is a bookshelf or perhaps the Bible at your bedside. Flowers may be here today, gone tomorrow, so skip them unless you have a bouquet which stays always in the same spot, such as a dried flower arrangement.

5. *Avoid overcrowding your set of loci* by trying to remember too many lists at a time. One per day is enough to start with. Although it works like a blackboard, with the newest list "erasing" the previous ones, your first attempts may stick much longer in your memory because you will spend more time and effort on them. In time and with more new lists smoothly recorded, these first lists will subside. If at first two objects instead of one come out of one of your loci, don't be too upset. Just identify the old and the new and go on. If you want to remember several lists on the same day, use different places for separate lists. For example, for 12 supermar-

ket items, use your first 12 loci; then for 5 things to do, use your next 5 (13–18).

Trial Exercise

1. Make a list of your loci on a separate sheet of paper. Number them clearly. Next to them write and number a shopping list (two lists side by side).
2. Visualize your first place and your first item. Make a clear image association of the two together. (For example, imagine the carrots you need overflowing the mailbox.)
3. Spend some time visualizing the two items together. You should end up with a short story tinted with emotion: humor, outrage, surprise, whatever.
4. Close your eyes and comment on your image association. Then proceed to the next item. The whole process will take about 15 seconds for each item.

Quick Review

1. The loci system makes it easy to remember a list in order.
2. It works like a blackboard and holds information for 24 hours.
3. Based on image association, it consists of associating an item you want to remember with a familiar place. Visualizing the two together is the key (the same principle is used for remembering names and faces).
4. Since your list of permanent loci follows a natural order, it is easy to retrace it at will.
5. Visualize the first item in the first place, the second item in the second place, and so on.

6. A mental walk through your loci will give you back your list of things to remember.

Exercises

Exercise 1:   Practice List: Packing for a Trip

Write this list vertically and place it next to your list of loci. Visualize the first item in the first place and continue until the end. Reclaim this list by reviewing your loci: (1) passport, (2) driver's license, (3) traveler's checks, (4) plane tickets, (5) address book, (6) camera, (7) toiletries, (8) hair dryer, (9) shaver, (10) umbrella, (11) bathing suit, (12) medications, (13) earplugs, (14) walking shoes, (15) water heater coil, (16) detergent, (17) inflatable hangers, (18) jeans, (19) sunglasses, and (20) house keys.

Exercise 2:   More Lists

The following lists are to be studied gradually. Start with list 1 and try to memorize 10 words with the loci method. Then add five more. Finally, try the 20 items together. Do the same with list 2. Try remembering 15 items with list 3 and then adding the last 5 items.

List 1	*List 2*	*List 3*
1. Log	Dog	Hog
2. Turkey	Matches	Sand
3. Elephant	Dish	Spoon
4. Fork	Book	Magazine
5. Computer	Flower	Grass
6. Straw	Ivy	Bee
7. Towel	Cave	Pine
8. Fire	Fog	Popcorn
9. Change	Coins	Rain
10. Misfortune	Father	Rye bread

11. Foot	Hand	Scratch
12. Dentist	Doctor	Surgeon
13. Fire	Wind	Plug
14. Mental	Double	Cute
15. Disk	Spine	Pickle
16. Tub	Nun	Nurse
17. Wine	Bourbon	Horse
18. Cross	Star	Lawn
19. Triangle	Square	Circle
20. Anger	Fear	Love

Once you feel comfortable with such miscellaneous lists, try using the system as a social game. Ask friends to name objects one at a time. Give yourself time to visualize them in your loci. Then retrace your steps. The objects will pop out. Later you will be able to recall them by number, which is even more impressive.

Exercise 3: How to Remember Recipes (or Instructions) with the Loci Method

Cornish Game Hens with Papaya (or any other exotic fruit)

1. In the first place, visualize the birds smeared with a paste made of margarine and curry powder to taste. (Visualize the process of mixing the ingredients and smearing the birds as well as the finished product.)

2. In the second place, visualize the smeared birds going into a 375° oven. (Visualize the number 375 in bright red on the oven door.)

3. In the third place, visualize a small bowl in which you have mixed chutney and lime juice to taste. (Set a timer for 30 minutes and visualize the sauce mixture being poured over the birds when the timer rings.)

4. In the fourth place, visualize a ripe, golden papaya cut up in cubes and added to the birds as a garnish just until heated: 20 minutes after adding the sauce. (Set the timer

again for 10 minutes only and visualize the cool papaya getting warmer and warmer around the birds.)

5. In the fifth place, visualize the rice pilaf ready to be served with the birds.

NOTE   Go over it again, making sure you get the timing right. It takes 1 hour total cooking divided in three steps: what you add after 30 minutes, what you add after 50 minutes, and what you serve it with.

This is only one example of how you can use the method. You could try dividing the recipe into more loci. I find it practical to group steps as I did above, because in a single image association it is easy to visualize at once several ingredients put together. You can get a very accurate picture of the consistency, color, and smell of the mixture. It also provides you with a dynamic picture of how to make the recipe. This works well for most cooks. Try it next time you watch a cooking demonstration on TV or when visiting a friend who enjoys cooking. (Make sure you write it down within 24 hours.)

Exercise 4:   Daily List Learning

Each day write down a list and describe how you went about memorizing it. Read and visualize your loci before starting. You should know them well. On your first trials you can look at your list of loci when placing and recalling the items to be remembered. Soon you will not need to check. Start with 10 items, then 15, then 20. In addition to learning a list each day, you should also write down how you went about doing it and what difficulties you encountered. There are some sample lists in this chapter, but choose your own. You will have more motivation to remember them better.

Practice with things to do, shopping lists, a list of your assets, a list of items in your safety deposit box, your worries, your blessings, etc. Take your pick! This should be more interesting to you than the test lists you also want to work on for practice.

It is important to use the systems at every opportunity, because they train your memory. Just like good observation skills, they can become part of your life. Daily practice guarantees easy success, and *by using your memory you will avoid losing it.* In the field of gerontology, a motto travels through every area of research: "Use it or lose it."

CHAPTER 11

Reading for Keeps

"There are books to be tasted, others to be swallowed, and some few to be chewed and digested."

Francis Bacon

Wouldn't it be wonderful to be able to remember everything you ever read or studied? Perhaps, but I am not so sure. Certainly you have come across a lot of printed matter that is irrelevant or that may have been relevant once but is not any longer. Memory works to meet one's present needs. Still, there are people who seem to be so well read as to have an inexhaustible file of references on all subjects. What is so special about them?

Such people have an unusual intellectual curiosity and an ability to study the mechanics of things. They are sensitive to all kinds of stimuli that activate the memory. They are selective and have the flexibility to choose how much effort to put into remembering something. Their filing system is well organized, and from multiple files they have access to multiple memories. Above all, they consult those files constantly, because their minds are very active. The perfectionists among them complain about their memories in a most unjust way, like the French Renaissance writer Montaigne, who was unable to appreciate his wonderful associative memory. Since he rebelled against rote learning, he knew few texts by heart. Yet his culture was immense—you just have to read his *Essays* to realize that. His motto was "Better a well-made head than a well-filled one."

Even people with excellent memories remember only a fraction of what they read, and it seems to be more than enough. But then, they are better readers. They work on what they read by pausing to think about it, commenting on it, taking notes, and reworking and reorganizing the material they find so interesting. They all have one passion in common: the urge to understand the world around them. Mortimer Adler in *How to Read a Book* points to the importance of reading critically and candidly with the purpose of understanding: "When we read for *information,* we acquire facts. When we read to *understand,* we learn not only facts but their significance." This is precisely what helps memory.

If you want to remember what you have just read, you must keep your mind on it a little longer in order to fix the memory. This requires some pleasant effort and a certain know-how based on new applications of general principles we have already learned.

Studies at the Carnegie-Mellon Institute for Learning have shown that "the differences in performance in the classroom that we observe are not so much a function of differences in IQ as they are *differences in strategies* for acquiring information." This means that according to *how* we read, we learn more or less. Thus pedagogy, or the art of teaching, does make a difference. By applying theory to life, by relating new knowledge to experience, we learn better. Rather than merely accumulating facts, we should *think* about them and try to understand them. Modern researchers have verified the idea that understanding is one of the bases of learning and memory. Experiments have proved time and again that unless one makes sense of the information, one cannot learn it. This is why numbers are remembered with codes, or systems. Senseless words are soon forgotten because they are not processed at a level that guarantees long-term retention. As we have seen throughout this book, searching for meaning is the key to depth of processing.

Yes, you can learn to read more efficiently. How? By setting your mind on an active course, asking questions, organizing the material as you read it, pausing to ponder the main idea, and finally reviewing it in a creative way. *Immediately after reading* is the best time to discuss the material, elaborate on it, and rework it in accordance with your aim. If you just want to retain an idea in order to mention it to a friend, you will not need the same time and effort as you would if you were studying for an exam. Even so, it is normal subsequently to forget material you never refer to. For example, you may have known a lot about chemistry, literature, or airplanes at one time, but having lost your major interest, it may seem to you that nothing is left. Sure enough, there is no trace of it in your active daily files (the blue zone), but traces of it *are* buried in the gray zone. If you have recorded the material in a systematic way, understanding the basic principle, you will be able to retrieve it when an occasion calls for it. From there, you will be able to recall more through deduction and other logical mental operations. If you recorded examples, or illustrations of the principle, they will come back as image associations.

Culture is a cumulative learning process. As we encounter something new, we integrate it with what we already know. Because recognition memory is very good, we pick up easily on something we once studied. It is easier to relearn something because we already have a reference file to refer to. All this is true provided that we have learned it well in the first place. Cramming for exams may be efficient on a short-term basis, but it does not stand the test of time. The best students study regularly and in depth; they give the material time to settle. They integrate it into their previous knowledge in an organized way. They are not rolling stones; they gather moss. They are more "cultured." As they add knowledge, they review what they know so that they have more active files in memory than the average person. After many years we remember only what we have learned methodically and in depth and what moved us most. A combination of emotional and intellectual skills does wonders for memory. You can verify these statements by asking yourself which classes, authors, and teachers you remember best.

Trying to remember everything you read is impossible and impractical. However, it is both practical and possible to work on remembering what interests you most for the specific purpose of sharing it with someone else while it is relevant, that is, not too long after the event. Normally, 48 hours after reading, people remember only about 20 percent of what they have read, and only the main ideas. To improve these odds, you must follow a pattern of *awareness* and *analysis*. There are things you can do before, during, and after reading to facilitate recall.

Before you start reading, help your concentration by getting rid of sources of distraction and interference. Turn off the radio or TV; get away from your demanding pets and children if you can. If not, wear earplugs. Also, setting a time goal will prompt you to read more intensely. Make sure you stick to it.

First, I will show you how to integrate imagery and visualization into your reading habits, thus following the basic information-processing model: from the sensory and emotional channels to the intellect. Then I will present a general principle plus specific questions to help direct your mind toward what is most important (task-oriented thinking). Finally, I will propose an easy, reliable learning strategy, the SQ3R. Each of the four sections will be followed by exercises to apply each individual method. Later you may want to use them all together. I am convinced combining these techniques gives much better results.

Imagery Method: A New Perspective on Reading

You have seen throughout this book how imagery and visualization enhance memory and how imagination helps in the process of building images. Applying this to reading is easy and rewarding. Using visualization and your imagination, you can get a clear image of what the story is about. Using organization gives you the final guarantee that you will file your memories in a way most likely to facilitate recall. You can organize what you visualize in a series of scenes in a specific order.

As a general rule, proceed from the images within a text toward the meaning they illustrate (from form to content). To do that, imagine your mind as a camera, recording everything in terms of images. The text thus becomes a screenplay with scenes, characters, action, and plot.

1. Visualize the text as you read. Focus on the specific situation, feelings, and mood. These concrete images will be ideas come to life that can be grafted onto the characters and plot.

2. Notice how one image is followed by another and how one scene follows another. Think in terms of a series of specific images.

3. Visualize this series of images in the sequence in which they appear in the text. Make a conscious note of it as you read and afterward. You will record the structure of the piece through imagery.

4. Ponder the originality of the author, his or her particular vision. Images reflect style. They convey powerful messages. Consider how they affect you. Comment.

Exercise 1:   Reading with Imagery

Start with the following texts and then choose texts which interest you. Visualize as you read, with scenes and images in mind. When you have read through the whole text, write down as many images as you can remember. Note them as precisely as possible as they pop into your mind. When this is done, try to reconstruct the sequence of scenes as they appear in the text. Check yourself by glancing back over the text. Notice what you missed but also what you remembered and continue applying this method to whatever you read. It takes time to develop new reading habits, but you will love reading through imagery. Vivid scenes will remain in your memory for years to come, as will the distilled essences of the texts. You will remember specific images and words. The style of the writer and his or her particular vision rather than just the writer's themes will reveal themselves to you. (Students in literature especially can benefit from this method.)

The Poor Boy's Toy

by Charles Baudelaire

(Translation by Danielle Lapp)
I want to offer a suggestion for an innocent diversion. There are so few pastimes which are not blameworthy. When you leave the house in the morning with the firm intention of strolling along the main streets, fill your pockets with those inexpensive small devices such as the flat jumping jack manipulated by a single string, the blacksmith striking the anvil, the rider with a horse whose tail is a whistle, and offer them to the neglected and poor children you meet in front of taverns where they stand by a tree. You will see their eyes grow immoderately big. At first they won't dare take anything. They won't believe in their good fortune. Then their hands will grab the present avidly, and they will run off like cats who go far away from you to eat the piece of food you gave them. These children have learned to distrust man.

On a road, behind the iron gate of a large garden at the end of which you could see the whiteness of an attractive castle lit up by the sun, there stood a beautiful fresh-complexioned child, dressed in those country clothes so full of fastidiousness.

Luxury, freedom from care, and the habitual display of wealth makes those children so gorgeous that they seem made from a different substance than the children of an undistinguished or poor class.

Beside him on the grass lay a magnificent toy, as splendid as its master, varnished, gilded, dressed in purple, and covered with plumes and glittering beads. But the child was paying no attention to his favorite toy. This is what he was looking at:

On the other side of the iron gate, on the road, in the midst of thistles and nettles, there was another child, dirty, frail, sooty, one of those child-waifs whose beauty an impartial eye might discover if, as the eye of a connoisseur guesses the ideal painting under a body varnish, it peeled off the repulsive patina of poverty.

Through the symbolic bars separating two worlds, the main road and the castle, the poor child was showing his own toy to the rich child who was greedily examining it as if it were a rare and strange object. Now, this toy which the small ragamuffin was irritating by shaking a wire box back and forth, was a live rat! The parents, for economy's sake doubtless, had gotten the toy from life itself.

As the two children laughed fraternally at one another, they showed teeth of a *similar* whiteness.

The Fox and the Stork

A fable by Aesop

Once a stork asked a fox to dinner.

So he fetched a pitcher of milk, stood it on a stone, put in his beak, and drank the milk. When he pulled out his beak to breath air, a few drops of milk dripped off, which the fox licked up.

When the stork had drunk well of the milk, he said to the fox, "Have you drunk your milk, brother? Have you had your fill?" "I have," said the fox, "and I want you to be my guest tomorrow, and eat with me."

And, just as they had said, they met the next day, very early, in a rocky place. The fox, in his turn, brought a pitcher of milk. He took it to a flagstone, broke it on the flat surface, and the milk ran out over the stone. The fox fell to and licked it up, while the stork beat his beak on the stone to no avail.

Then the fox asked, "Well, brother, have you drunk your milk? Had your fill?"

"Ah, brother, you put one over on me!"

"I only gave you back, brother, as good as you gave me."

Memorizing Poetry

Although any text can be visualized, poetry is ideal for reading through imagery. Poems are made of images (metaphors) which strike the imagination, move the senses, stir the mind, and beg to be remembered. Here are a few for you to enjoy.

Exercise 2:   Learning a Poem

1. Read the first stanza of the first poem *aloud,* concentrating on the images in it.

2. Close your eyes and try to visualize it.

3. Go on to the next stanza. Read it aloud and visualize it. Continue until you have read and visualized the whole poem.

4. You should have a clear picture of the images the poem contains. Check yourself by reading the whole poem aloud. This time the imagery will form in your mind, reinforcing the idea.

5. Try to reconstitute the poem by using its imagery. Close your eyes and visualize the *images* you remember. Write them down in the *words* you remember.

6. Check yourself by reading the poem aloud again. Correct the images if necessary by looking closely at the poem. Correct the order in which you presented them if you want to challenge yourself.

7. Last but not least, be aware of the sound of words. Be aware of rhythm and rhyme.

Exercise 3:   Telling about the Poem

Tell a friend or relative about the poem, first describing it and then expressing how you feel about it.

Exercise 4:   Memorizing the Poem

Finally, you may want to try to memorize the poem. Use the *cumulative learning* method: Learn one stanza a day, always reviewing the preceding ones as you add a new one. Try to integrate everything you have learned so far—visualization, mood, context, emotional involvement, sensory awareness—

and learn the poem the way an actor would, rehearsing it with
thought and feeling.

The Intimidated

Black in the snow and fog,
By the large vent-grating which is lighted up,
Their behinds in a circle,

On their knees, five children—poverty!—
Watch the Baker making
Heavy golden bread.

They see the strong white arm kneading
The gray dough and sticking it
Into a bright hole.

They listen to the good bread cook.
The baker with a fat smile
Mumbles an old tune.

They are nestled down, not one moves,
At the fumes of the red vent
As warm as a breast;

When, for some midnight feast,
Made like a brioche
The bread is brought out,

When, under the beams dark with smoke,
The sweet-smelling crust sings,
And the crickets,

When that warm hole breathes out life,
Their souls are so happy
Under their rags,

They feel so renewed with life,
The poor Jesuses covered with frost,
That they are all there,

Gluing their small pink snouts
To the grating, muttering things
Through the holes,

In stupor, saying their prayers
And crouching before this light
From heaven opened up again,

So hard that they burst their pants
And their shirts flutter
In the winter wind.

Arthur Rimbaud, 1870
(Translation by Wallace Fowlie)

To a Cat

Stately, kindly, lordly friend
   Condescend
Here to sit by me, and turn
Glorious eyes that smile and burn,
Golden eyes, love's lustrous mead,
On the golden page I read.

All your wealth of hair
   Dark and fair,
Silken-shaggy, soft and bright
As the clouds and beams of night,
Pays my reverent hand's caress
Back with friendlier gentleness.

Dogs may fawn on all and some
   As they come;
You, a friend of loftier mind,
Answer friends along in kind.
Just your foot upon my hand
Softly bids it understand.

A. C. Swinburne

She sights a Bird—she chuckles—
She flattens—then she crawls—
    She runs without the look of feet—
Her eyes increase to Balls—

Her Jaws stir—twitching—hungry—
Her Teeth can hardly stand—
She leaps, but Robin leaped the first—
Ah, Pussy, of the Sand,

The Hopes so juicy ripening—
You almost bathed your Tongue—
When Bliss disclosed the hundred Wings—
And fled with every one—

Emily Dickinson (poem 507)

Le Pont Mirabeau

Under the Pont Mirabeau flows the Seine
    And so our loves
Must I remember once again
The joy came always after pain

    Night falls the clock will sound
    The days go by Im still around

Hand in hand we lean and face to face
    While flows beneath
The bridge of our embrace
The river tired of lover's gaze

    Night falls the clock will sound
    The days go by Im still around

Love leaves us like this flowing stream
    Love flows away
How slow life seems
How violent the hopeful dream

Night falls the clock will sound
The days go by Im still around

Let the weeks and days run on
   Neither the past
Nor lovers gone return again
Under the Pont Mirabeau flows the Seine

   Night falls the clock will sound
   The days go by Im still around

Guillaume Apollinaire
(Translated by John C. Lapp)

Reading for Ideas and Personal Meaning

GENERAL PRINCIPLE   Proceed from the general to the
particular details.

1.   Note first things first: the subject or topic and the main
     ideas. Look for the essential message: What is this text
     about?

     - *Pause* on the title, subtitle, table of contents, quota-
       tions, or any cue given by the author. They all con-
       tain the main ideas.
     - Raise questions: They stem from the main ideas.
     - Embark on a *quest* to answer them as you read and
       after reading.
     - *Follow the thread* of the main idea. Notice how it
       develops and how it is illustrated. It is like Ariadne's
       thread, leading you out of the labyrinth. Hang on to
       it and you will not get lost in digressions and super-
       fluous detail.

2.   Note the most striking details: images, words, dialogue,
     characters. Consider the way in which the message is
     conveyed: How does it touch you?

- While you read, note the key words, images, and examples which illustrate the main idea. Become aware of the originality of thought, the beauty of the expression, and the impact they have on you.

3. Analyze the structure of the passage you have been reading. How many paragraphs are there? Usually there is one idea per paragraph. Find it and write it down. It can become the title of the paragraph. Looking for a title forces you to summarize the idea.

- The main ideas determine the structure. Ariadne's thread has shown you the way. Just review the different steps and get a perspective on the whole text.

Before you start reading, you must have an idea of what you are getting into. The subject will determine how much concentration and organization the reading will require.

During reading, you should look at the main idea close up. Read actively, looking for striking details, words, and images and becoming aware of how the text affects you.

After reading, you must recapture the main idea and how it is conveyed and comment on the text if you find it worthwhile. The skill you develop in reviewing will largely determine how well you remember the text.

Exercise 5:   Reading with a General Principle

Write down a brief commentary on every text you want to remember, following the preceding guidelines. Start with the ones I selected for you in this chapter. On the *first* reading, look for the main ideas and be aware of the key words and images. Group them as you go. Get a feel for the text. On the *second* reading, look for structure and details. Get a deeper understanding of the text. Pause after each long paragraph and ask yourself some questions about the text: Did you like it? Why or why not? How did it affect you? Did the author make his or her point? Do you agree with the author? Comment.

My Rival

I go to concert, party, ball—
  What profit is in these?
I sit alone against the wall
  And strive to look at ease
The incense that is mine by right
  They burn before Her shrine
And that's because I'm seventeen
  And she is fourty-nine.

I cannot check my girlish blush,
  My colour comes and goes.
I redden to my finger-tips,
  And sometimes to my nose.
But She is white where white sould be,
  And red where red should shine.
The blush that flies at seventeen
  Is fixed at fourty-nine.

I wish I had her constant cheek:
  I wish that I could sing
All sorts of funny little songs,
  Not quite the proper thing.
I'm very gauche and very shy,
  Her jokes aren't in my line;
And, worst of all, I'm seventeen
  While she is fourty-nine.

The young men come, the young men go,
  Each pink and white and neat,
She's older than their mothers, but
  They grovel at Her feet.
They walk beside Her 'rickshaw-wheels—
  None ever walk by mine;
And that's because I'm seventeen
  And she is fourty-nine.

She rides with half a dozen men
   (She calls them "boys" and "mashes"),
I trot along the Mall alone;
   My prettiest frocks and sashes
Don't help to fill my programme-card,
   And vainly I repine
From ten to two A.M. Ah me!
   Would I were fourty-nine.

She calls me "darling," "pet," and "dear,"
   And "sweet retiring maid."
I'm always at the back, I know—
   She puts me in the shade.
She introduces me to men—
   "Cast" lovers, I opine;
For sixty takes to seventeen,
   Nineteen to fourty-nine.

But even She must older grow
   And end Her dancing days,
She can't go on for ever so
   At concerts, balls, and plays
One ray of priceless hope I see
   Before my footsteps shine;
Just think, that She'll be eighty-one
   When I am fourty-nine!

Rudyard Kipling

A Lesson to Errant Wives

by Margaret of Navarre

King Charles, the Eighth of his name, sent into Germany a gentleman named Bernage, lord of Sivray, near Amboise, who to make good speed spared not to journey by day nor night, and so one evening came very late to a house and asked there for lodging. At this great difficulty was made, but when the master understood how great a king he served, he entreated him not to take in bad part the churlishness of his servants, since, by reason of certain kinsfolk of his wife, who were fain to do him a hurt, it was necessary that the house should be under strict ward. Then the aforesaid Bernage told him the reason of his embassage, which the gentleman offered to forward with all his might, and led him into his house, where he honourably lodged and entertained him.

It was now supper-time, and the gentleman brought him into a large room, bravely hung with tapestry work. And as the meats were set upon the table there came a woman from behind the tapestry, of a most surpassing beauty, but her head was shorn and the rest of her body was clothed in black gear of the German fashion. After that the gentleman had washed his hands with Bernage, water was borne to the lady, who when she had washed her hands sat herself down at the bottom of the table, without a word from her or to her. My lord de Bernage looked at her very attentively, and she seemed one of the comeliest women he ever had beheld, save that the manner of her countenance was pale and melancholic. And when she had eaten a little she asked for drink, and this was brought her by a servant in a most marvellous vessel, I would say a death's-head with the eyes closed up with silver, and so from this she drank three or four times. And her supper having come to an end she washed her hands, and with a reverence to the lord of the house she returned behind the tapestry without a word to anyone. Bernage was so astonished to see so strange a case that he fell into a thoughtful melancholy, which being perceived of the gentleman, he said to him: "I know well that you marvel within yourself at what you have seen done at this table; and for that I judge you to be an honourable man, I will not conceal the affair from you, to intent that you may not think there is so great cruelty in me without a weighty cause. The lady you have seen is my wife, whom I loved as man never loved before, so much indeed that to wed her I forgot all fear and brought her here by force against the will of her kinfolk. And she in like manner gave me so many evident proofs of her love that I would have risked ten thousand lives to bring her here as I did, to the delight of the pair of us, and we lived awhile in such quietness and contentment that I esteemed myself the most fortunate gentleman in all Christendom. But while I was away on a journey made for the sake of my honour, she so far forgot her virtuousness, her conscience, and the love she had for me, that she fell in love with a young gentleman whom I had brought up in my house and this I perceived upon my coming home. Yet I loved her so well that I was not able to distrust her till experience gave belief unto my eyes, and with them I saw what I feared more than death. Then was my love turned to madness and my trust to despair; and so well did I play the spy upon her that one day, feigning to go out, I hid myself in the room which is now her dwelling-place. And very soon after she saw me go, she went away and made the young man come to her, and him I beheld handling her in such fashion as belonged to me alone. But when I saw him get upon the bed beside her, I came forth from my hiding-place, and, taking him between her very arms, there put him to death. And since the offence of my wife seemed to me so great that death would not suffice for her punishment, I appointed one that I deem is much more bitter than death to her: namely, to shut her up in the room where she had her greatest pleasures of him she loved more than me, where I have set all the bones of her lover in an aumbry [a kind of chest], as a precious thing and worthy of safe keeping. And to the end that in eating and drinking she may not lose the memory of him, I have made serve her at table, with the head of that villain in place of a cup, and this in my presence, so that she may see living him whom she has made through her sin a mortal enemy, and dead for love of her him whom she preferred before me. And so at dinner and supper she beholds the two things which should most make her to despair; the living enemy and the dead lover; and all through her own sin. For the rest, I treat her as myself, save that she goes shorn, for an array of hair doth not belong to a woman taken in adultery, nor the veil to an harlot. Where-

fore her hair is cut, showing that she has lost the honour of
virginity and purity. And if it be your pleasure to see her, I
will take you there."

To this Bernage willingly agreed; and they went down
the stair and found her in a fine room, sitting alone before a
fire. Then the gentleman drew a curtain that was before a
high aumbry, and in it were hanging all the bones of the
dead man. Bernage had a great desire to speak with the
lady, but for fear of the husband durst not do it. He, per-
ceiving this, said to him: "An it please you say anything to
her, you shall see how admirably she talks." Forthwith
Bernage said: "Mistress, your long-suffering and your tor-
ment are alike great. I hold you for the most wretched of all
women." The lady, with tears in her eyes, graciously yet
most humbly answered him: "Sir, I confess my sin to be so
great that all the ills the lord of this place (for I am not
worthy that I should call him husband) can bestow upon
me, are as nothing compared with my sorrow that I have
done him a displeasure." So saying, she fell to weeping
bitterly; and the gentleman took Bernage by the arm and led
him away. And very early on the morrow he went on to
execute the charge given him of the King. But, in bidding
the gentleman farewell, he could not refrain from saying to
him: "Sir, the love I bear you, and the honour and privity
you have used towards me in this your house, constrains
me to tell you that, in my opinion, seeing the repentance of
your poor wife, you should have compassion on her. Fur-
thermore, you being still young have no children, and it
would be a great pity that such a brave line as yours should
come to an end, and they for whom, perchance, you have
no great love, should be your heirs." The gentleman, who
had resolved never again to speak to his wife, thought for a
long while on what my lord de Bernage had said to him, and
finding him to be right, promised that if she continued in her
humble repentance he would one day have compassion on
her. And so Bernage went forth on his embassage. And
when he was returned to the king his master, he told him
the whole matter, which the prince, having made inquiry,
found to be as he had said. And among other things,

Bernage having spoken of the lady's beauty, the King sent his painter, John of Pairs, thither, that he might draw her to the life. This he did, and with the consent thereto of the husband, who, beholding her long repentance, and having a great desire for children, took pity on his wife, who with such humbleness had borne her punishment, and, taking her back to him, had of her many brave children.

from *A Renaissance Storybook,*
Selected and edited by Morris Bishop.

This story is Nouvelle 32 of the *Heptameron.*
(Translated by Arthur Machen)

Reading for Specific Answers: The Five W's + H

Here is an easy method to help you find the main ideas, the details, and the structure of any text you read or any movie you watch. Try to answer the Five W's + H: *Who* did *what, when, where, why,* and *how?* This is a method taught in schools of journalism to make sure that students cover every aspect of a story. You can use it to focus your attention on a conversation, a radio program, or any important message.

Exercise 6:   Reading with the Five W's + H

Read the following story with these questions in mind: *Where* and *when* does the story take place? *Who* are the protagonists? *What* happens? *Why? How?* Pause and answer them as you go.

How Candide Was Brought Up in a Noble Castle and How He Was Expelled from the Same

In the castle of Baron Thunder-ten-tronckh in Westphalia there lived a youth, endowed by Nature with the most gentle character. His face was the expression of his soul. His judgment was quite honest and his mind extremely artless; and this was the reason, I think, that he was named Candide. Old servants in the house suspected that he was the son of the Baron's sister and a decent honest gentleman of the neighborhood, whom this young lady would never marry because he could only prove seventy-one quarterings, and the rest of his genealogical tree was lost, owing to the injuries of time. The Baron was one of the most powerful lords in Westphalia, for his castle possessed a door and windows. His great hall was even decorated with a piece of tapestry. The dogs in his stable-yards formed a pack of hounds when necessary; his grooms were his huntsmen; the village curate was his Grand Almoner. They all called him "My Lord," and laughed heartily at his stories. The Baroness weighed about three hundred and fifty pounds, was therefore greatly respected, and did the honors of the house with a dignity which rendered her still more respectable. Her daughter Cunegonde, aged seventeen, was rosy-cheeked, fresh, plump and tempting. The Baron's son appeared in every respect worthy of his father. The tutor Pangloss was the oracle of the house, and little Candide followed his lessons with all the candor of his age and character. Pangloss taught metaphysico-theologo-cosmolonigology. He proved admirably that there is no effect without a cause and that in this best of all possible worlds, My Lord the Baron's castle was the best of castles and his wife the best of all possible Baronesses. " 'Tis demonstrated," said he, "that things cannot be otherwise; for, since everything is made for an end, everything is necessarily for the best end. Observe that noses were made to wear spectacles; and so we have spectacles. Legs were visibly instituted to be breeched, and we have breeches. Stones were formed to be quarried and to build castles; and My Lord has a very noble castle; the greatest Baron in the province should have the best house; and as pigs were made to be eaten, we eat pork all year round; consequently those who have asserted that all is well talk nonsense; they ought to have said that all is for the best." Candide listened attentively and believed innocently; for he thought Mademoiselle Cunegonde extremely beautiful, although he was never bold enough to tell her so. He decided that after the happiness of being born Baron of Thunder-ten-tronckh, the second degree of happiness was to be Mademoiselle Cunegonde; the third, to see her every day; and the fourth to listen to Doctor Pangloss, the greatest philosopher of the province and therefore of the whole world. One day when Cunegonde was walking near the castle, in a little wood which was called The Park, she observed Doctor Pangloss in the bushes, giving a lesson in experimental physics to her mother's waiting-maid, a very pretty and docile brunette. Mademoiselle Cunegonde had a great inclination for science and watched breathlessly the reiterated experiments she witnessed; she observed clearly the Doctor's sufficient reason, the effects and the causes, and returned home very much excited, pensive, filled with the desire of learning, reflecting that she might be the sufficient reason of young Candide and that he might be hers. On her way back to the castle she met Candide and blushed; Candide also blushed. She bade him good-morning in a hesitating voice; Candide replied without knowing what he was saying. Next day, when they left the table after dinner, Cunegonde and Candide found themselves behind a screen; Cunegonde dropped her handkerchief, Candide picked it up; she innocently held his hand; the young man innocently kissed the young lady's hand with remarkable vivacity, tenderness and grace; their lips met, their eyes sparkled, their knees trembled, their hands wandered. Baron Thunder-ten-tronckh passed near the screen, and, observing this cause and this effect, expelled Candide from the castle with several hard kicks in the behind. Cunegonde swooned; when she recovered her senses, the Baroness slapped her in the face; and all was in consternation in the noblest and most agreeable of all possible castles.

Voltaire, *Candide* or *Optimism,* Chapter 1.

The SQ3R Method: A Learning Strategy for Serious Reading

During World War II, this method was devised to train people to acquire study skills quickly. It could be labeled "how to study better in less time more efficiently." It proved to be so successful that it remained in use in many college curricula. This learning strategy boasts an 80 percent recall after 8 hours versus the normal 20 percent. It tackles the process of forgetting by focusing on what interests you, selecting the main ideas, and reviewing the text with the structure in mind. It is based on the principles mentioned above, but there are specific steps to follow. SQ3R stands for

S = survey

Q = question

$$3R = \left\{ \begin{array}{l} \text{reading} \\ \text{reciting} \\ \text{reviewing} \end{array} \right.$$

Exercise 7: Reading with the SQ3R Method

Choose a text or a book that interests you. It is important to be motivated for maximum concentration. To start you can use the texts in this chapter, or you may choose to learn a specific chapter from this book, such as Chapter 2, "How Memory Works." Apply the SQ3R method as follows.

- *Survey* the text to get a general idea of what it is about.

- *Question* by rephrasing the titles or headings into questions and thus embark on your quest to find answers in the text.

- *Read* with urgency, actively looking for the main ideas, which are the answers to your questions.

- *Recite* those main ideas to yourself, pausing at the end of a long paragraph. Take brief notes.

- *Review* immediately to recapture the main ideas and the order in which they are presented (structure). Check your notes. You should have an outline. Fill in the supporting details. Verify your notes by glancing over the whole text to reinforce your learning. Notice what you missed but also what you remembered. Last but not least, express your comments and criticism: Have the questions raised been answered? Make sure you understood the author's point of view. Measure his or her statement by its context, replace it in its own perspective, and see if it stands. Look for objections, misinformation, prejudice, and bias.

You can adapt this method to your needs by skipping the reciting step. The survey of newspapers, magazines, reviews, and books will save you time and effort: You will focus on what interests you most. You must realize how important it is to review your readings *immediately:* You can seal the memory only by discussing and commenting right after reading. Take the time to recollect your thoughts when the text is fresh in your mind: You will remember more. Go beyond agreeing or disagreeing with the author. Try to say why you do and describe precisely what you like or dislike. You will be developing your critical sense as you become a better reader. If you tell your friends about your readings, you will keep your readings longer in your active file.

Quick Review

1. Reading more efficiently is reading for keeps.
2. Visualize what you read with the imagery method.
3. Read with a general principle. Look for ideas and personal meaning and proceed from the general to the particular details of your choice.
4. Read for specific answers: Five W's + H.
5. Learn easily with the SQ3R method.
6. Review your readings *immediately* by sharing your comments with others.

CHAPTER 12

Numbers

"You can't depend on your judgment when your imagination is out of focus."

Mark Twain

In this chapter we are going to apply everything we have learned so far to numbers. Image association is a technique which generalizes easily once you have integrated it into your way of thinking. Remember, there is no miracle about memory, just efficient mental operations.

How often have you felt frustrated at not being able to remember the number of a building you were going to, the license plate number of a dangerous driver, or your aunt's phone number? Even if you hate numbers, which is of course the major reason why you don't bother to give them your attention, you can find a system that suits you and enables you to remember them. You will have to take it as a game and try it before rejecting it as too complicated, weird, or time-consuming.

It has long been proved that mnemonic devices are strong aids to memory. Many people do not know about them; a few use them at school under the guidance of good teachers. (For example, the word "HOMES" is a first-letter mnemonic for the great lakes: Huron, Ontario, Michigan, Erie, and Superior.) Once they stop being students, they discontinue using them because the necessity is no longer there. Others, thinking they could not learn them, do not even try. Still others hide their laziness or insecurity behind skepticism.

I think I was one of those. It took me time to learn and practice the system I like. Now I even use it as an intellectual game to challenge my memory. Since motivation comes first, give yourself a stimulating goal. Pick out the number of something you always wanted to remember, perhaps the number of your bank account or your best friend's phone number. It is a well-known fact that people who remember numbers are interested, even fascinated by them. They may use one of several systems.

The most basic and most widely used system is *chunking,* which consists of splitting the thing to be remembered into several sections. It can be a number, a sentence, or a paragraph. That is the way social security numbers, account numbers, credit card numbers, and telephone numbers are written and spelled out. The mind registers small units of information better, combining them together. It is an easy way to organize material. It reminds me of the simple principle of using small pieces of thread when sewing. It may appear bothersome to make a knot, cut the thread, and thread the needle again and again, but that's the best way. Legend has it that the devil, that fallen angel always eager to prove his superiority, laughed at God, who was sewing with small pieces of thread. He challenged God to a race. The devil, beaming with self-confidence, undid the spool, certain he could use only one long piece of thread. He soon was caught up in all kinds of tangles without being able to make a single stitch. A blush of anger and shame on his face, he abandoned the competition. Likewise, we are bound to fail if we try to remember long numbers without dividing them into chunks. The mere repetition of the sequence of chunks may be sufficient: That's how you know your own phone number and the ones you use constantly.

Visualizing the number also gives excellent results. That's the way photographic memory works. People who have developed it visualize as easily as they breathe. In addition, many analyze the number, subdividing it in some kind of logical mathematical calculation. For example, to remember 10248, break down the number into 10 and 2 and multiples of 2—$2 \times 2 = 4$, $2 \times 4 = 8$. This seems very simple to mathematically minded people, but for those who dislike arithmetic and have no natural bent for these operations, systems based on imagery are much more effective. Numbers can be converted into concrete symbols which can then be combined into image associations. In this chapter you will have an opportunity to use your imagination. You will notice that behind the systems lie principles familiar to you:

- Replacing an abstraction with a concrete image
- Making an image association using visualization
- Weaving a context by creating a little story around the association

In order to make numbers easier to remember, only a few symbols are needed, usually 10. Then you combine them in a little story unique to this number. According to whether you are more verbal or more visual, you may choose one system or another; people who are very good at remembering numbers can use both types of systems. Read the chapter first to familiarize yourself with the variety of techniques. Then make your choice or come up with your own system if you are creative.

Fixed Associations and Codes

Verbal people are sensitive to sound and interested in words. Instinctively they find rhymes, puns, or other verbal analogies. They may find it useful to remember a reference list such as the following:

one = sun	seven = raven
two = shoe	eight = V-8
three = tree	nine = mine (a coal mine)
four = door	ten = den
five = hive	eleven = heaven
six = sticks	twelve = elf

In order to remember such numbers in the same way one remembers a name and face, one forms an association between the number and what is being counted. To form longer numbers, one puts together a combination of these simpler numbers. For example, if you want to remember the flight number of a plane, 328, using the above reference list you will have

$$3 = \text{tree} \qquad 2 = \text{shoe} \qquad 8 = \text{V-8}$$

Combine the numbers with a story association. Imagine a tree with a pair of shoes dangling from its branches and in one of them visualize a can of V-8 juice. Notice that while making your story you will want to keep the images in order: first, tree; second, shoes; third, V-8. The whole picture = 328 = your flight number.

Visual people can visualize very easily, and they remember what they see: shapes, geometrical figures, colors. Clear images come to their minds. For instance, thinking of a baseball team as nine players, they can actually see them in the field. Therefore, they may want to use another reference list which appeals to their visual sensitivity.

one = a long, straight pole

two = twins

three = a triangle

four = a square

five = the Pentagon

six = a six-pack of beer

seven = the seven dwarfs

eight = a can of V-8

nine = a baseball team

ten = your fingers

eleven = a pair of dice

twelve = a dozen eggs

These visual items can easily be associated with the number in question and can be used to form story associations. For example, to remember the flight number in the previous example, form a story association with a triangle instead of a tree and twins instead of shoes; V-8 is common to both codes. Visualize a triangle from which hang twins quarreling about a can of V-8. Too far out? Perhaps, but it will stick in your memory. With practice, you will find it easy to trace back 328 from this little scene. Try it with the following exercise.

Trial Exercise: Visual or Verbal Number Recall

Using either the verbal code or the visual code, make the necessary associations to remember the number of items in the following list. For example, you want to remember that there was *one* single cow in a barn. First you choose the visual or verbal reference list. Then you imagine the following:

1. Visual: a cow standing near a long, straight pole
2. Verbal: a cow standing under the scorching heat of the *sun*

This image should trigger recall of number 1 = one cow. Adding a personal comment such as "funny cow scratching herself against the pole" or "poor cow suffering from heat exhaustion" includes emotion and context and therefore reinforces the memory trace.

PRACTICE LIST:

One cow	Seven tape recorders
Two cars	Eight light bulbs
Three shirts	Nine rings
Four typewriters	Ten glasses
Five soldiers	Eleven lakes
Six pencils	Twelve doves

Now cover the list and write down the numbers of the different items given above; that is, how many objects of each category were there? The items were shirts, doves, soldiers, pencils, tape recorders, cows, rings, lakes, typewriters, light bulbs, and glasses.

These codes are often referred to as the peg system because you can "hang" things on them as we did in the loci system. The following section describes a few more techniques mentioned by Young and Gibson. As you will see, they sometimes combine visual and verbal associations.

Coding Systems

Numerical Code and Visual Analogies

Through logical analogies, each number refers to an image association.

1 = t (1 looks like t: a straight line with a bar)
2 = n (n has 2 bars)
3 = m (m has 3 bars)
4 = r (r is the last letter in "four")
5 = L (L is the sign for 50 in Roman characters)
6 = G soft like j, ch, sh (6 looks like a capital G)
7 = K, hard G, q (K looks like a vertical bar and a seven turned like this: <)
8 = f, v (in script, f has two loops like 8)
9 = p, b (9 looks like p reversed and b upside down)
0 = z, s (0 is zero)

To remember a number, convert it into consonants and then fill in missing vowels to form meaningful words. Use your imagination and do what you did for names: Say the consonants aloud until they ring a bell. For instance, let us take a phone number:

$$4 \ 7 \ 2 - 3 \ 8 - 1 \ 2$$
$$r \ k \ n \quad m \ f \quad t \ n$$
raccoon   move   tin

Going about it in a systematic way helps.

1.   Copy the consonants corresponding to the numbers.

2.   Start inserting vowels in alphabetic order: *ra, re, ri, ro, ru.* Here the first one rang a bell in combination with the third: *ra, k, n* reads easily as "raccoon."

3.   Think about all the possible vowels before deciding on the best in terms of context. I tried *maf, mef, mif, mof,*

muf but did not find anything, so I switched from f to v (its phonetic cousin): *mav, mev, miv, mov*—Tilt! I found a word with meaning.

4. Make up a little story as you go along. "Raccoon move" is fine. Your last choice of vowel will be determined by this context. Spontaneously, you might choose "tin" because it fits nicely. (*Tan, ten, ton, tun* might have fit another context better.)

Just visualize "raccoon move tin" and associate it with the person whose phone number it is. To retrieve the number, convert the letters back to numbers. Of course, you will soon know the equivalents by heart. The more you practice, the quicker you will learn them.

Isn't it fun to stamp each person with a little story illustrating his or her phone number? If you are a skeptic, you may object, saying that I chose an easy number and that it might not prove as easy in some cases. This number just popped out of my head. Having tried the system with many numbers, I can tell you that it is rare to come across one without meaning. Imagination is the key to image associations. It only takes practice to develop it.

Phonetic Numeral Code

Each number represents the sound of a consonant or group of consonants which sound very close (e.g., t, d). It is derived from the visual code we have described. For each letter, there is a peg word to illustrate it. These words are short and do not contain another pronounced consonant in order to keep the sound pure.

1 = t → tea	6 = sh → shoe
2 = n → Noah	7 = k → key
3 = m → Mom	8 = v → V-8
4 = r → rye	9 = b → bee
5 = L → law	0 = z → zoo

You may have noticed that this system combines verbal and visual associations. For maximum efficiency, mnemonists combine many sensory modes. Synesthesia is the rare sympathetic triggering of more than one of the senses by a single stimulus. Those who regularly experience it usually have extraordinary memories. This is why you will do better if you both visualize and hear the sound of words. If you don't like these words, you can choose your own, provided that you choose one-syllable words and avoid inserting other consonants.

You can use this peg system as another system of loci for remembering a list in order. Just associate the first item with tea, the second with Noah, and so forth. After 9 you can combine the peg images; for example, 10 = 1 (tea) + 0 (zoo). So you might visualize a cup of tea at the zoo entrance. Or you can devise new associations; for example, 10 = 1 (t) + 0 (s) = Tass (the Soviet news agency); visualize Russian characters and a Soviet flag on a newspaper.

Other Codes to Choose From

These mnemonic systems based on codes of image association were developed in the seventeenth century. After that time, many books on the subject were written in France, England, and the United States. Here I shall present the codes selected by Young and Gibson. The first is based on visualization; the second uses the letters of the telephone dial. These are relatively simple systems which are easy to use.

Ten-Picture Method This code is based on visualizing each number in the shape of an object. Using your imagination, it is not difficult to visualize the following symbols.

1 = spear	6 = snake
2 = goose	7 = semaphore
3 = pitchfork	8 = hourglass
4 = sailboat	9 = snail
5 = spread hand	0 = dish

This method is ideal for memorizing short numbers quickly. Try it with phone numbers. For example, to memorize 856-3210, visualize an hourglass, a spread hand, and a snake, and then a pitchfork, a goose, a spear, and a dish. Spend some time visualizing these pictures in order: Imagine that they are a cartoon. Make up a little story to link the items in that order. Let your imagination lead you.

Telephone Alphabet   On telephone dials, each number except 1 and 0 has three letters printed above it. These letters were used as codes which proved handy to memorize. For example, all telephone numbers in Kearny, New Jersey, used to start with KE. Thus, there were only five numbers left to remember. In Paris, the first three letters stood for the name of a street or location (e.g., DAN = Danton, MOL = Molitor). People used to give a phone number saying the whole name: MOLitor-16-85. It was handy and colorful. In addition, it located the area on the map of Paris.

1 = (Q)*	6 = MNO
2 = ABC	7 = PRS
3 = DEF	8 = TUV
4 = GHI	9 = WXY
5 = JKL	0 = (Z)*

NOTE   Letters (*) you supply mentally because they are not on dial. One can remember them by thinking of 1 (Q) as IQ and 0 (Z) as OZ.

Examples:

687-5484	phone number
OUR-KITI	key phrase
726-3255	phone number
RAN DALL	key phrase

Practical Application
of Number Associations

One often has to remember numbers in one's daily life, and associations can make it enjoyable and easy. Say you want to keep in your mind that your lawyer's office is on the eighth floor. Choose your reference list and just imagine a can of V-8 and associate it with your lawyer. Visualize him or her sitting at his or her desk with a can of V-8 in hand.

The most important thing is to follow your spontaneous association and make an image linking object and number. You can use your reference lists or improvise with a strong, clear image. For instance, 8 might be your granddaughter's age. Visualize her in your lawyer's office, telling the lawyer that she is 8 years old, and you will remember which floor your lawyer's office is on when you are in the elevator.

To remember several numbers, analyze them separately and make associations between them. Say you want to buy a garbage can that should measure 10 by 12 inches for you kitchen. First, imagine its shape: a rectangle as seen from above. What kind of rectangle is it? Referring to the first list mentioned for visual people, the width equals your fingers and the length equals a dozen eggs: width = 10 fingers × length = a dozen eggs. Thus, you will remember the size of the garbage can you want to buy by image association: your fingers and a dozen eggs.

Free Personal Associations

We have seen how much easier it is to remember numbers when we make a concrete image association representing them. Using systems is the traditional way to go, but I have tried to extend the theory to personal spontaneous associations and have found that it works for me. Use your imagination to project concrete meaning onto numbers. For any number you want to remember, ask yourself, "Does it ring a bell?" Does it represent anything familiar to you? Say you want to remember the phone number 539-3689.

1. Look at the total figure.
2. Divide the number into three groups:

    539   36   89

    Do any of these groups ring a bell?
3. Following your imagination, make a personal association. *Spend some time doing so.* Be flexible and visualize 539 as 53 and 9 or 5 and 39 if you cannot associate 539 with anything. For me this number happens to prompt a historical association:

    39: World War II
    36: the French Popular Front (the left in power)
    89: the French Revolution (1789)
    —
    Three major upheavals

Which associations come to *your* mind? Perhaps you are 53, or your wife is, or you have a daughter age 36, or you got married in '39, or maybe your mortgage will be paid in '89.

Notice that with my association I have to add a 5 in front of 39. It is easy enough to do: I visualize my hand with five spreadout fingers, eager to stop World War II; 539 is a clear image association. Then I look at the three numbers 39, 36, and 89. I notice they are in reverse historical order, so I run back the time machine.

5: my fingers: hand raised to stop.
39: the Second World War, closely preceded by
36: a pacifist leftist government, and
89: the French Revolution.

All this may seem farfetched, but the fact is it works because you spend time making a number association that is unique to you. In this way, numbers lose their impersonality and leave a better memory trace. Associating numbers with personal images triggers recall. Look for story associations and you will find them. As W. Somerset Maugham said, "Imagination grows by exercise and contrary to common belief is more powerful in the mature than in the young."

Pure Visualization

Focused attention and visualization may suffice for remembering most short numbers. Pause and take a mental picture. Visualize the numbers in bright red against a white wall or in yellow neon against a dark sky. Make sure to flash it onto the screen of your mind for at least 15 seconds. Project the number where it belongs. It is easy to visualize it in its context. For example, for addresses: near the door, on a building, or to remember floors, in the elevator. Repeating the number aloud helps by introducing another sensory mode.

Quick Review

1. Image association generalizes beautifully. It is very effective when applied to numbers.

   a. Convert abstract numbers into concrete symbols. Choose the system with which you feel most comfortable.

   b. Try out spontaneous free associations.

2. Focused attention and visualization alone may do the trick, especially if you dislike the systems. But try them anyway. Like many things in life, they are an acquired taste.

Exercises

Exercise 1

Try to remember your license-plate number and those of your best friends and relatives, one at a time. Try several methods. (This way you'll see which one works best for you.) For example, learn your number with the ten picture method, another number with the free association method, and another with the visual code.

Exercise 2

Try to memorize your social security number with the method of your choice.

Exercise 3

Try to memorize your best friend's telephone number with the free personal association method. If you stall on this number, try another number or method of memorization. Give your imagination a chance: it takes some time and practice to think about something.

Exercise 4

Try to memorize important telephone numbers like your parents, doctor, emergency, lawyer, travel agent, etc. Choose your favorite method—and drill and review often. Use the numbers frequently.

Exercise 5

Try to remember prices of items with the visualization method. Simply pause and take a mental picture of the ticket on the item. Visualize the two together, commenting on the value. Compare with a similar item if you wish to increase the difficulty of the exercise.

Exercise 6

Choose numbers relevant to your daily life, and make it a point to remember them with the method of your choice. For example, numbers in street addresses, floor numbers, number of stones in a piece of jewelry, number of plants on a window sill, number of lamps in a room, etc.

Exercise 7

Try to memorize your checking and savings accounts numbers with the method of your choice.

Exercise 8

Try to memorize your driver's license number and your passport number with your favorite method. Later on you can try to memorize family members' numbers.

Exercise 9

Choose your favorite method to memorize your passcode number for an automated bank-teller machine.

Exercise 10

Make it a point when you travel to remember flight numbers or train numbers and precise time schedules with the method of your choice.

NOTE   You may find out that different methods work better for different length numbers. Keep your mind flexible.

By the way, you can use any peg system in combination with your loci, e.g., for highway 89, visualize an hourglass in your first place and a snail in your second place.

CHAPTER 13

Foreign Languages

*"The sum of human wisdom is not contained in any one language, and no single language is **capable** of expressing all forms and degrees of human comprehension.*

Ezra Pound

Foreign languages are difficult to learn for many people because they seem to have no common basis with their own native languages. There is a quantity of new forms which have to be memorized and no frame of reference with which to connect them. One can make this task easier by using observation and organizational skills. A good illustration is C. Peter Rosenbaum's self-help book *Italian for Educated Guessers*. By analyzing forms, Rosenbaum shows how anyone can find principles to help him or her memorize foreign languages with a minimum of rote learning. Mere observation can turn you into an educated guesser. It is challenging, and it works.

As with any other knowledge, we shall compare the new with what we already know. Building a bridge between our culture and the new one is what learning a foreign language is all about. Next, you will see how visualization, sensory awareness, selective attention, image association, and weaving a little story in a context can be applied to learning a foreign language. Even relaxation will prove useful. Whenever you are anxiously searching for words in your attempt to speak the language, you will dare to speak more freely and therefore will be fluent sooner.

211

Visualization bypasses translation and provides an immediate concrete representation. Just visualize the object and repeat the word as accurately as possible. Or visualize a situation and act the part with the actual words and gestures. For example, in French "The sun shines" = "*Le soleil brille.*" Bypass the English words and concentrate on visualizing the sun shining in French while you repeat, "*Le soleil brille.*" Become aware of the quality of the sound: "*-leil*" and "*brille*" are shining sounds that radiate the sun's rays. I find the French sound more intense, and I associate it with the French temperament. All this is sheer speculation—I know it, you know it—but such personal comments are good for fixing a memory. In making them, I am using my sensory awareness and my imagination.

Selective attention comes next. Here the focus is on meaning and structure. A close-up of a word or idiomatic expression will provide several pieces of information with references to knowledge you already have. You will start opening files to store this new material in an efficient way. This is what people who know several languages have learned to do. A good teacher can help by showing you how to compare and study the differences between the new language and the native language, pointing out the common elements which are easily filed. An example would be to look for the stem of a word and see if you know it. It provides the core idea. For instance, the word "mankind" is more easily remembered if you analyze it (a combination of "man" and "kind") and then visualize a map of the world covered with men and women of every kind. Placed in a specific context, the word "kind," although a generic abstract term, takes on a concrete meaning more easily remembered. The equivalent in French is very close in structure and meaning: "*le genre humain.*" "Man" has two meanings in English: (1) male of the human species, as opposed to female, and (2) generic term for the human species. In French there are two words, one for each concept: (1) *un homme* and (2) *un humain.*

Sound and meaning Get into the habit of asking yourself whether a foreign word rings a bell in your own language. You are looking for resemblances between the two. "*Humain,*" for instance, sounds very close to "human," an adjective you often use in English. The French say "human kind." As for "*genre*," does it make you think of "gender"? Both have the same Latin root. Now focus on the differences. Once you have completed this analysis, all you have to do is learn the different endings. Visualize and spell out the words as you write them. In French, gender loses its d and becomes "*genre*"; "human" has an i at the end: "*humain*" as in "main." I cannot help making an association between "*main*" = "hand" and "*humain*": The hand is a unique trait of mankind. Thus I have woven an image association linking two different words into a neat context.

When you hear a new sound or word, try to get the correct pronunciation by finding a word in your own language that sounds similar. Some people do this automatically, and it helps their memory. It does not always work, and even when it does it is bound to be an imperfect approximation. Still, the layperson who is not used to foreign languages finds it helpful. Any reference point is better than none. For example, *la fiche* ("the file") in French sounds like the English "fish." You can go one step further and use image association to fix the meaning. Associate the ideas of "file" and "fish" and visualize a French file cabinet full of "*fiches*" in the shape of fish. It sounds crazy, but it works as a visual cue. Seeing the fish in the file cabinet, you will say, "Fish = *fiche*."

Vocabulary, which is the first stumbling block in learning a language, stems from a phonetic shock. We have to train our ears to the unfamiliar sounds. Next we must learn new ways to articulate them. Then we have to add meaning to the new words. Finally, we must study grammar, or the structure of the new language. This structure reflects the way the people in that particular country think. It is the key to understanding behavior and, often, point of view. The modern so-called direct method of teaching foreign languages immerses the student in the foreign language: No native word is ever spoken, so as to avoid translation (a more advanced exercise). Repetition of idiomatic structures is emphasized. The laboratory allows the student to drill until a structure is assimilated. This technique is based on mime and repetition. It can only be a complement to a course in which some basic rules of grammar and pronunciation are thoroughly explained and applied. Understanding, analyzing, integrating, and reworking are the mental operations that guarantee long-term retention. The fluency of expression comes with practice. It can be artificially maintained by drilling with tape recorders, but it gets standardized. It is easy to rattle off a fixed dialogue but difficult to improvise spontaneous answers to unfamiliar questions. Although you can build variety into the drills, only an actual conversation with a native speaker will provide a test of your fluency.

There are two major steps in learning a foreign language: *one passive and one active*. They correspond to recognition, a passive kind of memory, and recall, an active kind of memory which relies on cues and is therefore more difficult. In the first stage, you understand what is said and what is written to the point of feeling very familiar with the sounds, words, and structures. In the second stage, you participate, talking or writing with ease and thinking in the foreign language. From being passive, you become active. You will remain fluent only with practice, however. Thus, as the opportunity to use the foreign language decreases, you will have the impression of losing it. How quickly and thoroughly you lose it depends on how you acquired your knowledge. If you have a solid basis of understanding of the language and its structure, it will come back very quickly as soon as you are immersed in the culture. Without some formal learning it will prove much more difficult. For instance, two children of similar education each spent 5 years in South America between the ages of 4 and 9. Jane chose to perfect her knowledge in high school, learning grammar and reading, while Joe decided not to. Ten years later, only Jane could claim that she knew Spanish. Joe had forgotten almost everything. He could still understand a few words, but he found it more difficult to relearn the structures necessary to communicate.

According to how we process the information we want to keep in memory, we have a better chance of retrieving it. The best schools hire top teachers well versed in pedagogy as well as in their individual fields. Teaching how to think is teaching how to remember. Through mental operations we can retrieve some basic knowledge we may adapt to the new material we are learning. As the sixteenth-century French pedagogue Montaigne said, "Better a well-made mind than a full one."

Gathering vocabulary is an elaborate game similar to putting together a puzzle. After a while you just know how to spot the matching pieces. You have learned how becoming aware of your senses opens the way to observation; here you must listen openly to new sounds and become aware of how they affect you. This simple step may save you some trouble later. For instance, you may become aware of the fact you find the German sound *ch,* as in *hoch,* unpleasant and difficult to imitate. You will have to spend more time on something you resist. Look for an association in your own language and study the slight differences. You may get the right pronunciation by sheer imitation if you have a very good ear for music, but you probably will have to study more closely how this sound is produced by the native speaker.

Nowadays audiovisual material is available which makes this task possible at home. You can become very efficient at using it, provided that you follow some guidelines. Ask yourself if the new sound rings a bell in your own language. Then focus on the new sound and analyze it. For instance, the Spanish *o* is an open vowel, very different from the French *o,* which is closed. In Spanish you have to relax your lips and open your mouth; in French you must contract your lips and form a tight *o* with a minimal opening of the mouth. These phonetic remarks will help you, and you may become aware of them on your own if you analyze sounds carefully and compare them with sounds you already know. As you progress you will discover the different language families: Anglo-Saxon languages (English, German, Dutch), Romance languages (French, Italian, Spanish, Portuguese), Scandinavian languages, (Danish, Swedish, Norwegian), and so forth.

Once you know one foreign language, learning the next will be facilitated by looking for analogies, resemblances, and common points and filing them in the same place in your memory. You will realize that only the differences, the particularities of each language, constitute new learning. Classifying an item that is the same is a matter of becoming aware of something you already know. It will be easily recorded provided that you *pause* and make a point of noting the analogy. For instance, the Spanish *o* is the same as the Italian *o*. However, as we've discussed, it is different from the French and is more different still from the English *o*. As you ponder this, you may realize that there are actually two English *o*'s, or rather a British one and an American one. Neither is a pure vowel. Both are diphthongized; that is, they are colored by another vowel, *ou*, as in "boat." The British tend to exaggerate the *o-ou*, while Americans tend to downplay it. See how much you can teach yourself by mere observation?

In order to learn *idiomatic expressions*, verbs, and other words, get into the habit of analyzing them first as above. Then write them down on a sheet of paper and proceed to integrate them into a context through a little story. This works well for 10 words, though you may want to start practicing with 5. Suppose you are a foreigner learning English. Below is a list of new vocabulary seen in a textbook. First you must make sure you have understood their meanings in the context in which you found them. Then you want to put them into a new context, your own story association. Write a short paragraph integrating these new words together. The shorter, the better. For example:

to be aware of	to run after	so that
unpredictable	drought	the more the merrier
a mole	might have if . . .	soap opera

Read the list first and focus on the most difficult word. Here I think it is "soap opera." Once you find an idea to integrate the word, you are ready and the story will flow easily. Trust your imagination. Keep in mind that the purpose of the exercise is to bring these words to life in a context that will clearly illustrate their meanings. Just writing "Last night on TV there was a soap opera" is not enough. You have to specify what it is: "Yesterday on TV I watched a '*soap opera*,' a type of show originally financed and interrupted by advertisements of soap and other products. It was the sentimental story of an American family, who *was* not *aware of* the dangers created by *unpredictable* children: What will they think of next? During the *drought* it did not rain. The earth was dry and cracked, and *moles* were happily digging tunnels everywhere. They *might have been* thirsty *if* the children had not left a bowl of water in the garden *so that* they could come and drink. More and more came each day, and the children said, '*The more the merrier!*' The garden soon became a large playground where moles *ran* happily *after* one another.''

This exercise can be done at any level. Beginners will use simpler sentences and limited structures. It is interesting in a class situation to see the variety of stories which stem from a cluster of words. As the exercise is corrected, the meanings of the new words become clearer in the different contexts. Each student is then asked to write the correct version of his or her text and learn it well. Reviewing helps seal the memory and keep the meaning in context.

I find this to be one of the most effective exercises for language acquisition. You can improve it by visualizing the scene and saying the text aloud when you are learning it. You can do it alone, but ideally you should have someone to help correct your mistakes. *Never drill mistakes.* If you are learning a language, you probably have a teacher or know a native speaker who can help you.

Writing helps memory in many ways. It is a creative activity which integrates several mental functions. Since we remember better what we relate to, it is a good way to record something more accurately. Visual material such as pictures, videotapes, and diagrams can be used to bypass translation, which ought to be an advanced exercise only. As you look at the picture, fix memories directly in the foreign language. For instance, the idiomatic expression "Let's shake hands" translates into the French "*Serrons-nous la main*" ("Let's squeeze the hand"). You will hardly forget it if you learned it in the comic book *Asterix in Brittany*. The image of poor little Asterix the Gaul being vigorously shaken by his huge English cousin will stick in your mind forever.

Grammar is easier to learn when you draw diagrams which put all the forms of a given subject into perspective. Combined with the principle of replacing the word into a context, it is highly effective. You want to go back and forth from the whole picture to the specific detail, and you want to personalize the new material as much as you can. It has been pointed out that the most universally effective organizing strategy is the student's active search for patterns and principles or other significant relationships in the subjects he or she studies. That is why, apart from the rules, you should make your own connections. For example, in Romance languages the verb "to hope" must be followed by the subjunctive mode. French is an exception: *Espérer,* unlike other verbs expressing a hypothetical thought, is not followed by the subjunctive mode. Just visualize the French so sure of themselves that they think of their desires as realities. They hope in the mode of reality: the indicative. When they say, *"J'espère qu'il viendra"* ("I hope he will come"), they are sure he will. None of my students ever made a mistake with *espérer* after I suggested this association. You can make up your own using your imagination: It will be both effective and enjoyable.

Humor is particularly difficult to translate because it is often based on puns. Trying to explain a joke to a foreigner loses much of its flavor, but he or she can still grasp why it is fun in the original language. For example, consider the story of the 80-year-old California grandmother who after her first parachute jump said, "It's simply a case of mind over matter. If you don't mind, it doesn't matter."

All these principles should help you learn languages more efficiently and enjoyably. But please, if you forget something you never use, don't be angry with yourself—it is perfectly normal. Reread the paragraph on the memory storage system in Chapter 2, "How Memory Works." Nobody can actively remember what is buried and never referred to. A language you've "lost" will come back after a few days whenever you are immersed in the culture. Relax, knowing that you will have recorded it as well as possible.

Reading and listening to records and tapes are a good way of keeping languages alive in your active memory file.

Quick Review

1. Visualization bypasses translation: Think, see, and feel in the foreign language, saying the foreign word only.
2. Learn vocabulary and pronunciation by associating new sounds with familiar ones in your native language.
3. Write new words in context, making up a little story one paragraph long.
4. Compare structures, grouping the resemblances, isolating the differences, and focusing on the latter, which must be stored in a new file.
5. Be sensitive to sounds, nuances (e.g., vowel sounds), and idiomatic expressions. Awareness opens the gates of memory.

Exercises

Exercise 1

Remembering words in unfamiliar languages is easier when the image-association principle is applied. Choose street names or names of places. First listen carefully and look for a familiar meaning in your own language. Next analyze the different parts of the word and make a context story to remember it. Finally, say it aloud several times (with the right pronunciation, if you can) while you visualize the meaning. For example, a village in Germany: *Klosterreichenbach*. Suppose you don't know any German. Listen to the sounds and break up this long word:

sounds like . . .

Kloster-reichen-bach

cloister-ashen-bar.

Visualize a cloister built upon ash and a bar. As you remember the name of the village, you will begin to orient yourself in a country whose language you don't know.

NOTE   For languages with a different alphabet (Russian, Chinese, Japanese, etc.), you must get the words spelled-out phonetically in your own alphabet and then proceed to look for meaning in your own language.

Exercise 2

Learn vocabulary by integrating words into a story as mentioned above. Start with five words, then ten, up to fifteen. Have your pronunciation checked by a native speaker or a language teacher. Then learn it by rehearsing it and visualizing it several times.

Exercise 3

Improve your pronunciation by developing your listening and analytical skills as suggested in this chapter. Choose a number of words you find difficult. Get their right pronunciations and then analyze them, finding similar sounds in your own language, visualizing, etc.

Exercise 4

Rehearse useful sentences that you will need for your trip with the above suggestions. Listening to tapes by native speakers will help you immerse yourself in the sounds of the foreign language. For instance, some singers articulate well, and you may enjoy the music, too. In French, Georges Moustaki is a good example.

Exercise 5

Prepare yourself for your trip by reading foreign newspapers. Start at least 1 month before you depart.

Exercise 6

When abroad, reduce your anxiety and refresh your memory by devoting several days just to listening. That is, do not set an unreasonable goal of being accurate and finding the right words the first day you arrive in the foreign country. Accept your hesitations and tentativeness. They are normal. One good way of taking in as much vocabulary as possible is watching TV or listening to the radio. (I do that wherever I go, and I find that my active language comes back much faster because I am exposed to many more words than I would be in casual conversation.) A word of advice: Don't be too picky about the programs you select. What counts at this point is the language. Soap operas or movies are easier to learn from than the news, which is often rattled off in haste.

Exercise 7

Keep your foreign language fresh in your mind by reading regularly in that language. Magazines are fine for this purpose.

CHAPTER 14

Absentmindedness

"Habit diminishes the conscious attention with which our acts are performed."

William James

How to Cure Absentmindedness

Being absentminded means that your mind is absent at a time when it should be present. You are driven from one thing to another without any conscious control over what you are doing. You are distracted precisely when you should pause and reflect on what you are doing. The only sure way to fight absentmindedness is to become aware of the interferences that come between you and your goal. Then ignore the interference by continuing with what you were doing and refusing to give your attention to anything else.

Be One-Track-Minded

Say you are sewing in the living room and need your scissors; they are in the bedroom. You start walking through the living room and notice a stain on the carpet. Your cat comes along and meows. You pick her up and perhaps give her some food. When this is done, you realize you did not intend to feed the cat. What were you up to? You cannot remember. Only by going back to where you started—your sewing—do you recall by association that you need your scissors, which are in the bedroom. If you want to avoid another round of similar distrac-

tions, you will have to make a conscious effort to stick to your goal.

Pause on the idea of getting the scissors. Visualize them and think about where you will find them. By anticipating the scene, you will keep your mind occupied with what you want. If an interference appears, disregard it. (At first you may have to repeat to yourself, "Get the scissors," until you actually have them in hand.) *Do not stop* on your way to the scissors. The one-track-mind technique is very effective if you apply it systematically.

As people age, it becomes increasingly difficult to deal with interference in an efficient way. Rather than do several things at once, decide to do one thing well to the end. Do not allow yourself to stray from your original goal. Be one-track-minded and you will remember what is essential by bypassing interferences.

Do you have trouble remembering where you have parked? As you leave the car, pause and look around. Note the landmarks and visualize the road and your car. Read the name of the street or store close to you. This is the only way to get a clear image in your mind of where you are. Most people pay attention when it might prove very inconvenient to forget: at major airports or large parking lots. Keep the ticket with you at all times and get into the habit of writing on it the number of your parking area. This will give you peace of mind. You may surprise yourself. If you concentrate, you probably will remember the number without looking at the ticket. To ensure a better recording, visualize the color of the area where the elevators, staircases, and main pillars are. Look for anything that might orient you: a building you can see or a ventilation system. Be aware of what you see on the way out. Before entering the elevator or leaving the parking area, turn around and take a mental picture of this spot from the perspective you will have when you return. One of the reasons people lose their way is that they do not recognize the path when they reverse their steps. Indeed, a road or street looks different depending on which direction you go. (Scenic roads should be taken in both directions for that very reason.) Moreover, as you are busy

rushing or talking, you may not register anything of what you have seen because your mind is on something else. Develop your observation skills: Pause, think, and take mental pictures of key reference points. You will notice immediate results. You will remember directions and places, and generally you will gain a better sense of orientation.

Use Image Associations

Now it is time to apply the principle of image association to common forgetfulness. Remember how efficient it proved to be for faces and names and the loci? Well, it has many more applications. If you tend to forget where you put things and often leave important items in different places, this is a useful technique.

First, pause: Look at the object and where you put it. This becoming aware is the single most important step because it prevents you from performing an automatic gesture which escapes your consciousness. You will record that particular gesture. Next, make up an image association between the two. To cure repeated forgetfulness, make image associations with objects you are going to see whenever you need to remember something. One gentleman used to forget his portfolio wherever he went. This annoyed him considerably and forced him to spend a great deal of time looking for it. I suggested that he associate his portfolio with the seat of his car. He visualized it on the passenger's seat right next to the driver's seat where he usually sat, making a conscious image association of the two together. He also developed the reflex of looking at the seat nearby before starting the car. If the seat was empty, he had to go back and get the missing portfolio. He thus reduced the nuisance by becoming aware of his forgetfulness sooner.

Another example is a woman who always left her purse on the counter of department stores. She was told to develop the reflex of checking her hands before leaving a place. She was to associate hands and purse, visualizing them together. The pause made the whole difference. She interrupted her flow of actions and became conscious of finishing one thing before

starting another. Image association is a very powerful technique. Her hands became associated with anything she might be carrying: purse, bag, etc. She reported never losing her purse again.

I developed this useful habit and noticed additional benefits: It may prevent you from losing something. Before leaving a friend's home one evening, I checked my hands. I had my purse, but my gold bracelet was missing. I looked around and found it on the floor, where it had probably fallen while I was taking off my coat. I had spent the whole evening without noticing that my bracelet was not on my wrist. I'm sure I would have lost it had it not been for this conditioned reflex of image association.

A final example covers the problem of remembering which day of the week it is. Find a specific event that usually happens on one particular day and associate the event with the day. For example,

Monday 6 a.m.: Garbage collection.

Wednesday afternoon: Walk in the park.

Then, instead of looking for an abstract Monday or Wednesday when you want to know what day of the week it is, think of the specific event for each day: "Was I awakened by the garbage truck this morning?" Make your own calendar of daily events which recur regularly in your life. You can use TV programs if you like or any kind of structured activity. It can be meeting with a friend every Thursday for coffee or tea, practicing a sport, going to an exercise class, or playing bridge. You will notice how much easier it is to keep track of time this way.

Another approach is to use a list of symbols for each day. Make an image association between a symbol and an object you wear all the time, such as your wedding ring. Spend 1 minute each morning visualizing your wedding ring with the symbol for the day. Pause and think about the association. Every time you look at your ring, you will see your most recent image association. Here is my list of visual symbols which sound like the days. If you do not like these, make up your own.

Monday = moon	Friday = small fry
Tuesday = two twins	Saturday = Saturn
Wednesday = wedding veil	Sunday = sun
Thursday = Thor's hammer	

I hope that by now you enjoy using memory systems. If not, give yourself more time and continue to practice the principle of image association.

Use Visual Reminders

Forgetting something on the stove or in the washing machine can bring frustration and sometimes disaster. Using a timer with a bell will help if you are not hard of hearing. Another way is to place next to you an object which will remind you of what you want to do. For example, if you want to remember your laundry, leave the soap box on the table next to where you are reading or watching TV. Even if you cannot hear the machine stop, you will think about it soon enough when you see the detergent.

Place visual reminders in a prominent spot where you cannot miss them. Be aware that familiarity quickly replaces novelty so that new items blend into the background. When this happens, you'll fail to notice them even if they are right under your nose. For example, I had to use a skin product two nights in a row every week. Deciding on two regular days—Friday and Saturday—helped somewhat. But I had left the product on my vanity and soon became used to seeing it there. I missed seeing it twice on the evenings in question. I now place it *in the sink* on Friday and Saturday mornings. I can't miss it there.

If you have to move around a lot, a "memory pocket" may be the answer. You can place in your pocket small objects to remind you of other things. For instance, you might tear a piece off the top of the detergent box and slip it into your pocket. You might also carry a little pad and make notes as you go. Writing the date is helpful. You will have to develop the reflex of checking into your memory pocket often enough.

Do you tend to forget whether you have locked the door, turned off the gas or electricity, shut off the electric blanket, or turned off the sprinkler in the garden? Do you ever feel anxious and uncertain about such things to the point of having to go back and check? It may be that you lack self-confidence; you are in constant doubt about whether you have done the right thing. When you check, you find that everything is all right. There is a foolproof way to solve this problem. Become aware of your action at the moment you do it; visualize yourself making the movement in question and comment on it: "I am locking my car, all the doors are locked, and the hand brake is on." Here again it is the *pause* which is important. Interrupt your conversation or thread of thought and use monologue to make sure you are recording your action consciously. It is not silly to talk to yourself. Everybody does it all the time, but unconsciously and silently. Awareness makes a tremendous difference for recording memories. Think of it this way: Conscious episodes stand out against the numerous impressions you receive all through the day. As you think and comment about them, you leave a memory trace. When trying to remember whether you locked your car, you will see yourself doing it; you will hear yourself commenting on it. Imagery is a strong ally. Use it! Combined with awareness, it will give you the certitude you need to have peace of mind.

The same method will relieve your anxiety about misplacing objects. When we are busy, distracted, or in a hurry, we tend to do things without thinking. Our minds are on what we have to do next; therefore, we do not give our attention to an action we somehow already consider in the past. Although there is a reason for such behavior, you must recognize how inefficient it is. You waste more time looking for misplaced objects than you would recording your action consciously.

I used to rush and hide away such things as money and jewelry whenever a repairman or window washer came to my house. As I heard the bell ring, I would grab any valuables lying in sight and put them anywhere, the nearest place usually. I cannot say how many times I fumed at having "lost" something. My husband would take a more relaxed approach and calmly say, "Dear, you will find it someday. I'm sure you know it is not lost." Still, it was very irritating not to find what I needed when I needed it, so much so that I decided to apply what I teach.

First, I stopped rushing. After all, what's the hurry? Anyone will wait a couple of minutes at the door, and I have asked all my friends and relatives to let the phone ring at least six times to allow me to complete whatever task I am in the middle of. Second, I paused and visualized each object where I placed it, commenting on the image association: "I put my gold stud earrings, my chains, and my amethyst ring with my toiletries." It took only a few seconds, but when I thought "jewelry," the image association prompted me: I literally saw the different items in my toiletry case. Since I integrated this pause into my life, I am more relaxed and rarely misplace or "lose" anything. Many of my students feel the same way once they master the techniques. It is amazing how a few seconds of concentration and organized thinking can make a big difference. See for yourself!

How do you find a lost *idea?* By retracing your steps and looking for visual cues. If you were reading, reread the previous page. If you were walking, go back to where you were or retrace your steps mentally. If you were in conversation, backtrack to what was said. (Changing topics often triggers new ideas with looser logical associations. These spontaneous personal associations produce digressions, and digressions are the main cause of lost ideas.) Visualize the conversation, recalling who said what and reconstructing the chain of thoughts. Ask many questions and you will actively trigger recall. Be open and observant and you will find some visual cue. As you develop good observation skills, your recording will be more precise and the recall will follow suit. Feeling sorry for yourself when your memory fails does not help; relaxing and looking for visual reminders do.

Use Regular Fixed Places

There is nothing like order to help cure absentmindedness. If you tend to lose your keys, decide once and for all on one place to put them when you arrive home. It could be near the phone or on a special hook on the wall. When you are on the go, develop the reflex of putting them always in one special pocket of your jacket or purse. Choose one place and stick to it. Make sure you put them there consciously every time until it becomes a conditioned reflex. Although we want to avoid automatic reflexes in general, because they eliminate the pausing and thinking process, they are useful in the case of actions which recur time and again.

B. F. Skinner's Tips

At age 78 B. F. Skinner delivered a lecture called "Intellectual Management in the Later Years" to the American Psychological Association. Here is a digest of his useful reflections.

Do It Now!   Daily forgetfulness happens to all of us at times in our lives when we are worried or absorbed by work, grief, or any other strong emotions. Skinner gives a typical example of the kind of forgetfulness that irritates people so much because it can happen at any time: You forget to take your umbrella although you had decided to do so when you heard the weather report. You had the idea but did not follow through to help your memory by, for example, placing the umbrella in front of the door as a visual reminder. Train yourself to do things when you think about them. If you can, pay your bills the day they arrive; pledge your membership for your public television station as soon as you are reminded of it. Write to a friend when you are thinking about him or her. Pick up the phone and call the repairman now. Lose the unfortunate habit of procrastinating—through action. You will feel better about your memory and will reduce the guilt that often accompanies procrastination. Remember, a bird in the hand is worth two in the bush, so capture your ideas when they hatch. Use everything you have learned and add this basic principle: Do as much as you can to plant a cue at the time you think of it. Later it may be too late.

Prompt Yourself   We all search for words, especially when we are tired or anxious. But it is mostly when we get older that the frequency of such episodes becomes annoying. The reason is that words become less accessible with age. Skinner urges people to resort to "skillful prompting." You should plant verbal cues as you did visual cues. For instance, before going to a class reunion, review the list of people who will attend; before a concert, read the program. Use fill-in lines as "verbal padding" to give yourself more time to remember, for example, "As I was saying," "As you may well know," "At this point it is interesting to note."

Rehearse   If you want to say something specific to a friend over the phone, rehearse it before you pick up the phone. Use visualization and add gestures if you wish. Saying it aloud will add to the powerful effect of kinesthetic memory. Also, spend some time thinking about how the person will react. You will be less likely to lose the important message. Write it down if it is complex or if there are several messages and keep the note near the phone. Of course, rehearsing is a must if you want to give a speech or even say a few words in front of an audience. While rehearsing, you may become desensitized to fear of performing. When your expression becomes a reflex, you will have won the battle, according to a famous school of acting. You are less likely to lose your lines and vary your interpretation, thus ensuring a constant quality to your performance.

Rest Your Mind   For maximum efficiency, your mind should be rested when you undertake an intellectual task. Think of it as a muscle: It can perform only in alternation with relaxation. Skinner talks about the productive use of leisure. Leisure should be relaxing. It should be a change of activity. Whereas some activities—fishing, knitting, painting—are relaxing, others are not. Playing chess or reading an essay on political philosophy is not recommended for an intellectual who wants to take a break from demanding work. However, such activities may be quite appropriate when that person is on vacation or for a person who is not intellectually active most of the time. Many people do not realize how much strain they are putting on their minds, and they suffer from mental exhaustion. With age, we tire more easily and must learn to pace ourselves. "It may be necessary to be content with fewer good working hours per day," Skinner points out.

It is up to you to organize your life so that you create intellectual stimulation without straining your mental faculties. When you feel your ideas are not so clear or you are making mistakes, stop. Do something radically different: Watch television, go for a walk, read an easy novel, or take a nap. It will do wonders for you. A brilliant scholar used to take 10-minute naps when he felt stymied. After that he was able to resume his work as fresh as a daisy. He never seemed to strain, and he published constantly.

Understanding Absentmindedness

For those who want to know more about how and why mental lapses occur, I recommend a very interesting book entitled *Absent-M·nded?* by James Reason and Klara Mycielska. Did you notice something missing in the title? (There should be an ı under the dot.) Most people wouldn't, because the mind stretches to fill the gaps. This proves quite handy when we read newspapers full of misprints but not when we are editing a paper. Professors Reason and Mycielska have researched mental lapses and the absentminded slip. They found out that these lapses occur

- When we perform automatic actions or gestures
- When we are distracted or preoccupied
- In familiar and constant environments
- In people who are vulnerable to stress

- In older people because they are more sensitive to interference

Habit and familiarity diminish conscious attention. What are we to do, since habit and conditioned reflexes are helpful and yet are dangerous at times? Accepting small mental lapses as part of life seems the wise choice. We take the possibility of minor accidents in stride, hoping we will avoid the big ones. One thing is sure: We are more likely to avoid disaster if we develop reflexes of conscious awareness. They can prevent most catastrophic lapses or at least reduce their frequency. Routine checks, such as locking the house, should be performed consciously, not mechanically. The more we are creatures of habit, the more we seem doomed to mental lapses. Smile when you find yourself pushing someone else's cart in the supermarket but make sure your lights are off when you leave your parked car. Beware of familiar things you take for granted.

Frequency removes the need for attention. Combined with stress, anxiety, and fatigue, it can be disastrous. Whenever you embark on an important task, be aware. However, overattention as well as inattention may be a cause of error. For example, if you are driving and keep watching the speedometer, you may miss the police car riding next to you or, worse, a truck changing lanes abruptly in front of you. In other words, by focusing on only one thing you may fail to see the whole picture. This is how one misses the obvious. The solution is to record consciously each step of any important operation. As William James remarked, "An object once attended to will remain in memory whereas one inattentively allowed to pass will leave no traces."

Absentminded errors are often due to imperfect rationality rather than irrationality. In studying accidents (train, subway, plane), Reason and Mycielska noticed that they were all the result of a wrong assumption. For instance, in a plane crash at the Tenerife airport, the pilot of a KLM plane assumed that the runway was clear although the visibility was near zero. Why he did so and did not wait for the tower to give him clearance, we will never know. Or did he believe he actually heard the order he had been waiting for so long?

Errors of perception are common, especially when people are tired and under stress. We often hear what we expect to hear or want to hear. A London subway car slammed into the wall at an end station. It is probable that the driver had a mis-perception as he went through the last curve preceding the station. It was very similar to a previous one, which he must have forgotten for a fraction of a second: He simply assumed that he was somewhere else. Losing track of time or place is frequently a source of errors. These errors are more likely to happen as people get older. Rather than assume everything is all right, check and double-check, especially when you are anx-ious and tired.

A last example is the mystery of the Bermuda triangle, where a squadron of air force training planes was reported to have disappeared. Investigations proved that the planes ran out of fuel and plunged into the sea because they went in the wrong direction. The commanding pilot mistook one island for another and chose to think that his perception rather than his instru-ments was right. Nobody dared challenge his authority, be-cause they were inexperienced pilots. Similar plane accidents have occurred when copilots did not step in at a crucial mo-ment. Psychologists recommend a closer relationship between crew members as a way to reduce such incidents.

A last remark on accidents: Most of them are due to poor attention, poor judgment, or a combination of the two. If you've ever taken a safe-driving course, you probably learned that most accidents occur in familiar surroundings within 20 miles of home, where people know the roads and their normal defenses are down. You should recognize other situations inter-fering with attention: when angry, high, elated, drowsy, intoxi-cated, fatigued, or distracted. Be aware of the times when you may be vulnerable to such factors. If you can't devote your full attention to the important task, set it aside until you can.

What about losing track of conversations? It happens to us all when we lose interest, but it mainly happens to daydreamers, to narcissists more interested in what they themselves are thinking, and to older people for a different reason: As we get older, we tend to lose one type of control process by which we keep track of our progress through the routines of everyday life. We use recent information less efficiently. Older people are inclined to stick to some favorite theme even when it is no longer relevant to the present topic of discussion. In a study by Patrick Rabbitt at Oxford, young and older subjects were asked to listen to a taped conversation between several persons. Older subjects recalled fewer statements when they were made by more than one speaker. They did worse than young people when they tried to recall who had said what. Old people have excellent recall of what they themselves have said but seem to have little or no remembrance of the events which preceded their statements. This is also true for young people who are self-conscious for any reason.

You must make an extra effort to keep track—*if* it is worth it to you. That is up to you to decide. It could be listening to a debate or watching a play you want to discuss later on or just actively participating in a stimulating conversation. Stepping in and commenting on something you find interesting at the moment can be a good way of keeping it in mind. If you address the person who raised the point, you will remember that it was he or she who made it. But remembering what we say is the most important, for we can always ask others to repeat what they said. Nobody can keep track of everything, so try to keep track only of what matters most to you.

As a general rule, forgetting is normal when it does not occur too frequently. We select material to discard momentarily in favor of something else that steals our attention. It is best to accept a healthy balance of control and surrender to pleasant interferences. Life would be terrible if we could program ourselves all the time—there would be no surprises! Imagine what it would be like if everyone remembered every detail of the past. There would be no forgiveness, and the grudges we held would outweigh our positive feelings. We cannot choose to forget as we want, but we can remember most of what is important to us, provided that we help our memory. Now that you've learned how to help yours, go ahead and have faith in your new techniques.

It is also important to put your occasional memory lapses into perspective. Have you always been distracted, "in the clouds"? Recall episodes of forgetfulness that embarrassed you, creating unpleasant situations in the past. Do you tend to shift responsibilities onto friends, your spouse, or colleagues? Have you been so busy lately that there is always something you forget? Overloading memory is just as bad as underloading it: Both ways you lose. You can win most of the time by loading it skillfully. That's what this training is all about.

Quick Review

In order to fight absentmindedness, you can resort to several techniques based on pausing, awareness, and image association.

A. How to Cure Absentmindedness

1. Be one-track-minded (Complete one simple action at a time.)
2. Use associations (make image associations)
3. Use visual reminders (your memory pocket)
4. Use regular fixed places (a place for everything and everything in its place)
5. B. F. Skinner's tips:

- Do it now
- Prompt yourself
- Rehearse
- Rest your mind

B. Understanding Absentmindedness

1. "Habit diminishes the conscious attention."

2. Beware of
   - Automatic gestures
   - Familiar environment
   - Stress
   - Fatigue
   - Distractions
   - False assumptions

3. Check and double-check anything important.

Exercises

Exercise 1

Define your type of absentmindedness and make it a point to solve *one problem at a time*. Give yourself one week per item. Try the principles described in this book and see what happens. You should become more aware, more patient, and should start developing more strategies.

Exercise 2

Train yourself to become more aware by *pausing* before you go anywhere. Look around, think where you're going, what you need, and check that you have everything.

Exercise 3

Try to become aware of your automatic gestures. At first you will notice the gesture after the fact, but little by little you will able to catch yourself in time.

Exercise 4

When tired or under stress, pay twice as much attention to tasks. Better yet, postpone doing them unless you must at all costs complete the task now.

Exercise 5

Whenever you think of something you must not forget to do, try to do it right away. If you cannot, plant a cue to prompt yourself at the time and place you need to be reminded. Use both visual and auditory cues.

Exercise 6

Before you go to a party, class reunion, movie, or the like, review the names of the people you will be seeing and visualize them in the context in which you know them. If you are prepared, you will feel more relaxed and will remember more relevant information.

Exercise 7

Make it a point to remember directions next time you go to a new place. Take cues and mental pictures as you go and rehearse them.

Exercise 8

Check and doublecheck important instructions. Visualize the steps several times before actually performing the task.

Exercise 9

If you tend to do several things at the same time, choose priorities and try to do one thing after the other.

Exercise 10

If you are hopelessly absentminded—for instance, if you frequently put on unmatched socks—get into the habit of *pausing,* looking around, and asking yourself questions. This will help you develop an awareness of your surroundings.

Conclusion

In this book you have learned new ways of thinking about and improving your memory. Now you know how to identify mental attitudes and psychosocial changes affecting memory function. Memory is no longer a mysterious mechanism, and you can differentiate attention problems from retention problems. No longer do you blame your memory for your inattention. You have also learned how to increase your concentration through heightened awareness, relaxation, and selective attention. You have practiced using all your senses to form clear images of the things you want to remember. You have trained yourself to ensure a good recording through accurate observation and analysis. Finally, you have been using associations to set up cues for easy recall of faces, names, lists, numbers, and anything else you need to remember. You have seen that by integrating your emotional, sensory, and intellectual resources, you have gained control of your memory.

Keep in mind the general principles of memory training:

- Pause.
- Relax.
- Become aware.
- Select.
- Focus.
- Take mental pictures.
- Comment (with personal associations and emotions).
- Raise questions.
- Organize (in categories, principles, structures).

- Review.
- Use information (to keep it in your active storage file).

It is time for you to compare the way you feel now about your memory with the way you felt before you started this training. Take the memory test you took at the beginning of the book (p. 3) right now and compare your answers. I think you will be pleased with the results.

I hope you have enjoyed the journey. Continue applying the principles you have learned. Integrate them into your daily activities and keep up the good habits you have developed. Vary the rhythm as necessary but always challenge your curiosity and interest in life. Like a skillful gardener, you can now cultivate your memory with much joy and satisfaction.

Identifying Your Memory Problems

		Excellent			*Average*			*Poor*
a.	My memory in general	1	2	3	4	5	6	7
b.	Names and faces	1	2	3	4	5	6	7
c.	Appointments	1	2	3	4	5	6	7
d.	Where I put things, e.g., keys	1	2	3	4	5	6	7
e.	Words	1	2	3	4	5	6	7
f.	Things I have read	1	2	3	4	5	6	7
g.	Remembering what I was doing before an interruption	1	2	3	4	5	6	7
h.	What people tell me	1	2	3	4	5	6	7
i.	Places I have been	1	2	3	4	5	6	7
j.	Directions and instructions	1	2	3	4	5	6	7

For Further Reading

Adler, Mortimer: *How to Read a Book*, Touchstone Books (Simon & Schuster), New York, 1972. (reading)

Baddeley, Alan D.: *The Psychology of Memory*, Harper & Row, New York, 1976.

Bolen, Jean Shinoda: *Goddesses in Everywoman*, Harper & Row, New York, 1985. (personality and aging)

Cermak, Laird: *Improving Your Memory*, McGraw-Hill, New York, 1976. (imagery)

Ivanov, Serghei: *Les Mystères de la Memoire*, Editions MIR Moscou, 1977.

Lewis, David, and James Greene: *Thinking Better*, Rawson Associates (Scribner), New York, 1982. (organization and attitudes)

Loftus, Elizabeth: *Memory*, Addison-Wesley, Reading, Massachusetts, 1980. (distortions and eyewitness)

Lucas, Jerri, and Harry Lorayne: *The Memory Book*, Ballantine, New York, 1985. (mnemonics)

Nicholson, JoAnne, and Judy Lewis-Crum: *Color Wonderful I*, Bantam, New York, 1986. (sensory awareness)

Peters, Thomas, and Robert Waterman: *In Search of Excellence*, Harper & Row, New York, 1982. (motivation and success)

Proust, Marcel: *Remembrance of Things Past*, Random House, New York, 1981. (involuntary memory)

Reason, James, and Klara Mycielska: *Absent-minded?* Prentice-Hall, Englewood Cliffs, New Jersey, 1982. (mental lapses)

Robinson, Francis P.: *Effective Study*, Harper & Row, New York, 1970. (reading, SQ3R)

Skinner, B.F.: "Skinner at 78," Lecture given at 90th annual American Psychological Association, Washington, D.C., August 1982.

Watslawick, Paul: *The Situation Is Hopeless but Not Serious: The Pursuit of Unhappiness*, Norton, New York, 1983.   (identifying attitudes and behavior patterns)

Young, Morris N., and Walter B. Gibson: *How to Develop an Exceptional Memory*, Wilshire, North Hollywood, California.   (mnemonics)

Index